P9-DDN-568

STERLING BIOGRAPHIES

# SITTING BULL

## Great Sioux Hero

George E. Stanley

STERLING

New York / London
www.sterlingpublishing.com/kids

To Gwen.

STERLING and the distinctive Sterling logo are registered trademarks of
Sterling Publishing Co., Inc.

**Library of Congress Cataloging-in-Publication Data**
Stanley, George Edward.
  Sitting Bull : great Sioux hero / by George Edward Stanley.
    p. cm. — (Sterling biographies)
  Includes bibliographical references and index.
    ISBN 978-1-4027-5965-9 (pbk.) — ISBN 978-1-4027-6846-0 (hardcover) 1. Sitting
Bull, 1831–1890—Juvenile literature. 2. Dakota Indians—Biography—Juvenile literature.
3. Hunkpapa Indians—Biography—Juvenile literature. 4. Little Bighorn, Battle of the, Mont.,
1876—Juvenile literature. I. Title.
  E99.D1S6184 2010
  978.004'9752—dc22
  [B]
                                                                          2009024141

Lot #: 10  9  8  7  6  5  4  3  2  1
03/10

Published by Sterling Publishing Co., Inc.
387 Park Avenue South, New York, NY 10016
© 2010 by George E. Stanley

Distributed in Canada by Sterling Publishing
c/o Canadian Manda Group, 165 Dufferin Street
Toronto, Ontario, Canada M6K 3H6
Distributed in the United Kingdom by GMC Distribution Services
Castle Place, 166 High Street, Lewes, East Sussex, England BN7 1XU
Distributed in Australia by Capricorn Link (Australia) Pty. Ltd.
P.O. Box 704, Windsor, NSW 2756, Australia

*Printed in China*
*All rights reserved*

Sterling  ISBN 978-1-4027-5965-9 (paperback)
         ISBN 978-1-4027-6846-0 (hardcover)

Image research by Larry Schwartz

For information about custom editions, special sales, premium and corporate
purchases, please contact Sterling Special Sales Department at 800-805-5489
or specialsales@sterlingpublishing.com.

# Contents

# Events in the Life of Sitting Bull

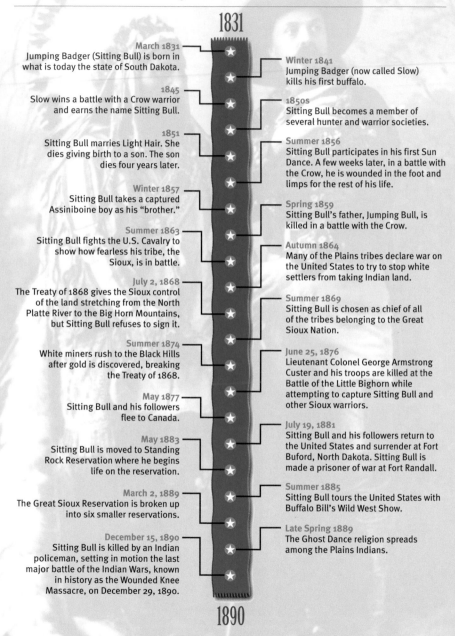

## 1831

**March 1831**
Jumping Badger (Sitting Bull) is born in what is today the state of South Dakota.

**Winter 1841**
Jumping Badger (now called Slow) kills his first buffalo.

**1845**
Slow wins a battle with a Crow warrior and earns the name Sitting Bull.

**1850s**
Sitting Bull becomes a member of several hunter and warrior societies.

**1851**
Sitting Bull marries Light Hair. She dies giving birth to a son. The son dies four years later.

**Summer 1856**
Sitting Bull participates in his first Sun Dance. A few weeks later, in a battle with the Crow, he is wounded in the foot and limps for the rest of his life.

**Winter 1857**
Sitting Bull takes a captured Assiniboine boy as his "brother."

**Spring 1859**
Sitting Bull's father, Jumping Bull, is killed in a battle with the Crow.

**Summer 1863**
Sitting Bull fights the U.S. Cavalry to show how fearless his tribe, the Sioux, is in battle.

**Autumn 1864**
Many of the Plains tribes declare war on the United States to try to stop white settlers from taking Indian land.

**July 2, 1868**
The Treaty of 1868 gives the Sioux control of the land stretching from the North Platte River to the Big Horn Mountains, but Sitting Bull refuses to sign it.

**Summer 1869**
Sitting Bull is chosen as chief of all of the tribes belonging to the Great Sioux Nation.

**Summer 1874**
White miners rush to the Black Hills after gold is discovered, breaking the Treaty of 1868.

**June 25, 1876**
Lieutenant Colonel George Armstrong Custer and his troops are killed at the Battle of the Little Bighorn while attempting to capture Sitting Bull and other Sioux warriors.

**May 1877**
Sitting Bull and his followers flee to Canada.

**July 19, 1881**
Sitting Bull and his followers return to the United States and surrender at Fort Buford, North Dakota. Sitting Bull is made a prisoner of war at Fort Randall.

**May 1883**
Sitting Bull is moved to Standing Rock Reservation where he begins life on the reservation.

**Summer 1885**
Sitting Bull tours the United States with Buffalo Bill's Wild West Show.

**March 2, 1889**
The Great Sioux Reservation is broken up into six smaller reservations.

**Late Spring 1889**
The Ghost Dance religion spreads among the Plains Indians.

**December 15, 1890**
Sitting Bull is killed by an Indian policeman, setting in motion the last major battle of the Indian Wars, known in history as the Wounded Knee Massacre, on December 29, 1890.

## 1890

# He Lived and Died for His People

*I wish it to be remembered that I was the last man of my tribe to surrender my rifle.*

Sitting Bull woke suddenly. The dream had seemed so real. As had happened in another long ago dream, the meadowlark had spoken to Sitting Bull, telling him how the end would come.

Just then, the door burst open and several men rushed in and began pulling Sitting Bull from his bed. They were Metal Breasts, Sioux policemen, whom Sitting Bull recognized as Shave Head, Red Tomahawk, and Bull Head. They pulled him outside where some of Sitting Bull's followers had gathered and were shaking their fists, demanding that their leader be released.

When the Metal Breasts ignored them, one of Sitting Bull's bodyguards raised his rifle and fired at Bull Head's chest. As he fell, Bull Head aimed his own rifle at Sitting Bull. Given Sitting Bull's ability to communicate with animals, it's easy to believe that he saw the rifle turn into a meadowlark, but now, when the meadowlark opened its mouth, instead of a song coming out, there was a bullet, headed right toward him.

In that instant, Sitting Bull must have thought: I have always tried to be a wise and compassionate leader. How did it come to this?

# CHAPTER 1

# The Greatest Gift

*When I was a boy the [Sioux] owned the world.*
*The sun rose and set in their lands.*

It was bitterly cold on that winter day in March 1831. There along the banks of the Grand River, in what is the present-day state of South Dakota, stood a cone-shaped, buffalo-hide tepee. Inside, a fire burned brightly, warming two women.

A child had just come into the world, and the mother, called Her-Holy-Door, was filled with joy at the event. As was the custom at all births, the old woman who had helped deliver the baby put it on a piece of soft deerskin, then cut the umbilical cord, releasing the child from his mother. She sprinkled a powder made of fungus on the infant's navel to keep it free from infection. Next, the old woman cleaned the baby with grass and rubbed buffalo fat all over his body to keep the skin soft. Finally, she wrapped the little one in a blanket made from the soft hide of a buffalo calf.

With her work done, the old woman laid the

Sitting Bull was born in a tepee such as the ones shown in this 1881 photograph of a Sioux camp outside Fort Buford, Dakota Territory.

baby next to Her-Holy-Door. After cleaning up, she stuck her head outside the opening of the tepee and told the father standing there that he had a son.

## A Gift from *Wakan Tanka*

The father was a warrior named Sitting Bull. He did not know then that one day his newborn son would also carry his name. Like all other Native Americans, Sitting Bull truly believed that a man's most valued possessions were not his horses or his weapons but his children, and a boy was the most prized gift a warrior could receive from *Wakan Tanka*, the Great Spirit, the supreme being who created the Sioux.

When Sitting Bull went into the tent to look at his son, he was almost at a loss for words to thank *Wakan Tanka* for this healthy child. As the father of a newborn son, Sitting Bull probably hoped that the boy would bring honor and glory to the Hunkpapa, their branch of the Great Sioux Nation. As it turned out, this would be exactly what happened. In fact, in later years, as an explanation of this special bond with his people, the boy would say, "I began to see when I was not yet born; when I was not in my mother's arms. It was then I began to study about my people."

Known as great hunters, the Sioux followed the buffalo herds back and forth across the Great Plains of what would one day be the United States of America. The Hunkpapa were also mighty warriors who greatly valued their independence. They were feared, yet respected, not only by all the bands of the Great Sioux Nation, but by the other Indian tribes of the region as well.

## Jumping Badger

Sitting Bull and Her-Holy-Door named the infant boy Jumping Badger for reasons we do not know. They both knew that their son would eventually receive other names, ones more appropriate and descriptive, after his personality began to develop.

During the first few days after Jumping Badger's birth, Her-Holy-Door rested, then a feast was held to honor the boy's birth. Everyone held him and told his parents how wonderful he was. Even though Sitting Bull knew that it was a traditional courtesy to do this, he still found himself beaming with pride at every remark.

*Everyone held him and told his parents how wonderful he was.*

One thing Jumping Badger was not allowed to do, though, from the day he was born, was cry. Each time the baby opened his mouth to do so, Her-Holy-Door would pinch his nose in order to stop any sound. She wasn't being cruel. This was simply a way to train a child from birth that such noises could put the Hunkpapa in danger. A baby's wailing could easily attract enemies of the tribe who would then attack the camp.

When Jumping Badger was two months old, Her-Holy-Door wrapped him in a blanket and put him in a wooden frame called a cradleboard which she strapped to her back. This allowed Her-Holy-Door to resume her duties in the camp and to have Jumping Badger with her at all times—especially if she was moving about.

When Her-Holy-Door stayed inside the tepee, performing chores such as cooking or sewing, she would lean Jumping Badger's cradleboard up against

Sitting Bull spent the first months of his life in a cradleboard similar to the one shown in this 1899 photograph of a Native American woman carrying a baby.

# The Great Sioux Nation

The people of the Great Sioux Nation lived on the Great Plains between the Mississippi River and the Big Horn Mountains of southern Montana and northern Wyoming. They ranged as far north as the Canadian prairies and as far south as the Platte River in what is now the state of Nebraska. In the last half of the nineteenth century, they were great hunters and warriors. There are three major groups divided by dialect and subculture: the Dakota, the Nakota, and the Lakota. These tribes still exist today.

They can be further subdivided into different *bands*—a term often used interchangeably with *tribes*:

1. Dakota: the Mdwekanton, the Wahpekute, the Wahpeton, and the Sisseton
2. Nakota: the Yankton and the Yanktonai
3. Lakota: the Brule, the Oglala, the Miniconjou, the Blackfeet, the Two Kettle, the Sans Arc, and the Hunkpapa

Although each band lived in its own separate village, several bands would sometimes hunt buffalo and fight common enemies together because, as kindred groups, they never felt any hostility toward one another. In fact, intermarriage was even quite common.

As shown in this map, the ancestral home of the tribes of the Great Sioux Nation stretched from Montana and Wyoming in the west to Wisconsin in the east.

one of the tepee's frame poles so her son could watch her work. In this way, the Hunkpapa believed, children started to learn about the daily activities of the tribe from a very early age.

When it was time for the tribe to move with the buffalo herds, Her-Holy-Door would hang Jumping Badger's cradleboard from her horse, along with the cooking pots and bundles of herbs.

## Slow

As Jumping Badger continued to grow, his personality developed, too, and it wasn't exactly what either Sitting Bull or Her-Holy-Door had hoped it would be. Jumping Badger never did anything in a hurry. If Her-Holy-Door handed him a piece of meat, he didn't immediately stuff it into his mouth, as most children would have. He held it in his hand, looking intently at it, almost *studying* it, before he finally ate it. In fact, Jumping Badger seemed to think about most things before he decided to act. This wasn't lost on other members of the tribe who began to call him "Slow" instead of "Jumping Badger." Sitting Bull and Her-Holy-Door accepted "Slow" as their son's second name and began calling him by it.

In 1836, by the time Slow was five years old, he was riding behind his mother on her pony whenever the Hunkpapa moved their camp. When he grew too big to do this, he was given his own pony.

Slow enjoyed life among the members of his tribe. During the summers, along with all the other boys and girls in the camp, he wrestled, swam in the rivers, and ran foot races. During the winters, he spun wooden tops on the frozen ice of the rivers and creeks. He also rode sleds made from buffalo hide wrapped around buffalo rib bones down snow-covered hills. Sometimes, if the snow was especially slick, these sleds would race past the

The Sioux loved sports, whether it was wrestling, swimming, running, or playing a game of lacrosse as shown in this 1851 painting.

finish line and into the camps, forcing people to scatter to keep from getting hit. The chaos probably caused Slow and his companions to squeal with delight.

But by 1841, when Slow was ten, he and the other boys his age no longer played with the girls. For one thing, the girls were busy learning skills from their mothers and grandmothers so they could be productive members of the tribe. There was a lot to learn, too, since the women were responsible for making fires for cooking, carrying water from the river to the camp, and scraping

Sioux women were responsible for the day-to-day chores of the tribe. This photograph from the late 1800s shows two Native American women performing some of those tasks—taking care of a baby, cooking a meal, and scraping buffalo hide to make soft and supple clothing.

buffalo hides with sharp rocks to make them soft and pliable for sewing. They also searched for wild fruits and vegetables to cook and serve along with the meat that the men brought back from hunts.

The men of the tribe taught Slow and the other boys how to become great warriors. Often, Slow's father and uncles would take him to a nearby stand of trees to search for the best type of wood from which to make a bow. They taught him how to cut the wood, how to polish it with a rock, and how to shape it slowly over a fire. When this

As this c. 1900 photograph shows, Native American boys started their training to become warriors when they were still very young.

process was finished, Slow was allowed to decorate the bow, using colored **pigments** and horsehair. Triangle designs represented tepees while straight lines next to ovals represented lances and shields. Slow also learned how to string the bow with dried buffalo intestines and how to make arrows with flint rock heads.

Still, even with his new knowledge, Slow was considered too young to go on an actual hunt, so he continued to play games with the other boys, knowing the day would soon come when he would be a warrior.

## War Games

One of the boys' favorite games was pretending to attack the camps of their mortal enemies—especially the Crow and the Assiniboine tribes. These tribes were historically known to encroach on land that the Sioux considered theirs. Warfare was an honorable way of life among many Native American tribes, and stealing was accepted as the best way to get what the tribe needed, especially horses.

In their pretend game, Slow and his friends would have hidden in the tall grass outside their camp, near the horse corral, and waited until one of the older boys guarding the animals was distracted by something. They then would have slowly but quickly crawled toward the gate. When they finally reached it, they would have given their loudest war cries to let the guarding boy know he was being attacked and the horses were being "stolen." Slow's group would then have raced back to the tall grass while the angry and embarrassed boy gave chase. Of course, in every one of their "attacks," Slow and his friends were always victorious.

But Slow knew what he and his friends had done was just a game. When real warriors returned from battle, they sang fighting songs with painted faces and eagle feathers in their hair. Slow vowed that one of these days, in the not too distant future, he himself would become the most fearless warrior of the entire Great Sioux Nation.

Little Eagle, a Sioux warrior, is shown in this 1900 photograph. His great ancestor, Sitting Bull, would have been dressed in a similar manner at the same age.

# Indian vs. American Indian
# vs. Native American

When Christopher Columbus sailed from Spain in 1492, he thought he was headed for India, but instead he reached the Americas. Columbus and his men thought the land really was India, so they called the native peoples "Indians." The name stuck. Unfortunately, down through the centuries, "Indian" was often used by non-native people in a negative sense, and brought to mind stereotypes, such as "blood-thirsty savages." In the 1960s, enlightened and more progressive Americans began using the term "Native Americans," not only to show respect for the original inhabitants of the United States, but to remove confusion with the indigenous people of India. It wasn't long, though, before the term "Native American" was also rejected by many people as being dry and bureaucratic. Russell Means, a member of the Lakota Sioux tribe and the founder of AIM, the American Indian Movement, prefers the term "American Indian," mainly because under the term "Native American" the U.S. government also includes American Samoans, the Aleuts, the original Hawaiians, and the Inuits, in addition to American Indians. What most American Indians actually prefer, when possible, is to be called by their tribal name: Apache, Cherokee, Comanche, Kiowa, or Lakota Sioux, to name a few.

# CHAPTER 2

# Becoming a Warrior

*I was born a warrior. I have followed the warpath ever since I was able to draw a bow.*

Although ten-year-old Slow constantly thought about being a great Sioux warrior—and was convinced that he could do what the other men did—his daily routine as one of the younger members of the tribe didn't change very much over the next few months.

When the buffalo moved, the Hunkpapa moved, often about twenty-five miles on an average day. If the buffalo seemed satisfied with a place to graze for a few days, the Hunkpapa would set up a new camp that was far enough away so that the buffalo wouldn't be frightened by them, but close enough for the hunting parties to chase them.

Just as the buffalo looked for sweet grass to graze, the Hunkpapa looked for a secluded spot near water and trees for their new campsite. Such a place would provide shelter from the fierce winds of the Great Plains during summer and winter, and from their enemies, especially the Crow to the west and the Assiniboine to the north.

The Sioux moved their villages when the buffalo moved, but they always tried to camp close to trees and water as depicted in this 1836 painting by George Catlin.

# Setting Up Camp

Once the spot was chosen, the leaders would smoke a ceremonial pipe to thank *Wakan Tanka* for leading the tribe to such a perfect place to camp and hunt. The Sioux believed that all good things that happened to them came from this respectful use of the pipe. It created the proper spiritual feelings for the Earth and all living things on it.

The women and the girls would then unfasten the tepee poles from the *travois*, a two-poled sled which the horses pulled from campsite to campsite, and set up the frames in a large circle. Next, they unfolded the buffalo hides and wrapped them expertly around the poles. The women always left an open space at the tops of the tepees so that the smoke from the cooking fires could escape. Once the fires were started by spinning the end of a stick in a small pile of dead leaves and grass heaped on a flat rock, the women of the tribe began preparing the meals.

To carry their belongings from camp to camp, the Sioux used a travois like the one shown in this photograph from the late 1800s.

# Inside a Sioux Tepee

A Sioux tepee was much like the tepees of other Indians of the Great Plains. It was made of several tall wooden poles that formed a frame, which was covered with buffalo skins. The skins were so tough that they kept out winter storms and summer heat. When the Sioux moved from place to place, they took their tepees along. The hides were folded up and put on wooden sleds, and the poles were fastened to horses so they could be dragged along the trails. The average tepee was twenty feet wide at the base. There was usually enough room inside for at least twelve people to sleep in beds—also made from buffalo skins and placed against the walls. Fur-lined skins usually covered the floor. In the middle of the tepee was a fire pit that was used for heating and cooking. Other than one or two backrests made from willow branches tied together and used by older members of the family, there was very little furniture. Food, clothing, tools, and weapons were hung from pegs on the poles framing the tepee.

When the Sioux arrived at their new camp, the first thing the women did was set up the tepees. Occasionally, in good weather, the buffalo hide coverings were taken down from the pole frame to let in fresh air, as shown in this 1891 photograph.

Slow especially enjoyed meat roasted over the open fires, whether it came from the buffalo or from the deer or from the many game birds on the plains. Her-Holy-Door and the other Hunkpapa women preferred boiling the meat. For one thing, it caused less smoke, and it also rendered a broth that could then be used for stews. No part of an animal was wasted, and it wasn't unusual for Hunkpapa families to eat boiled buffalo brains and tongues and to make soup from buffalo hooves and tails.

After each meal, but especially in the evenings, the elders would remain beside the fire to tell stories, either of the great deeds of famous Sioux warriors or of the tribes' different spirits. Slow always enjoyed hearing about how his warrior ancestors fought and defeated all of their enemies to make the Great Sioux Nation the most powerful among the Native people of the Great Plains. Afterward, as Slow lay in the darkness, wrapped in his buffalo blanket, with the tales he had just heard replaying themselves over and over in his mind, he would think about what he would do once he went into battle.

Whenever the Hunkpapa warriors were about to leave for a buffalo hunt, the women, the children, and the old men would sing their wishes for a safe and successful hunt. The warriors then rode their horses through the camp, chanting a song that asked *Wakan Tanka* to guide them to the big herds. Slow would always stand apart from the rest of the tribe as he watched this ritual, and wonder how long it would be before he was riding along with the warriors. He knew he was near the age when it could happen soon.

## First Buffalo Hunt

One winter morning when Slow awakened, he was told that he would be going with his father and his uncles and the other warriors of the tribe on his first buffalo hunt. Slow had already been taught by his father and his uncles how to ride his pony and how to make a bow and arrows. He had even hunted small game near the camp. But Slow knew that accompanying the warriors on a buffalo hunt was the true first step to becoming a Sioux warrior.

Based on Sioux hunting traditions, Slow probably mounted his pony alongside his father and his uncles, and faced the crowd that always gathered before a hunt to sing their wishes. Suddenly, he spied a boy a few years younger than he, looking at the warriors in the same way Slow had only a few weeks earlier. When the boy caught his eye, Slow raised his bow in a salute to let the boy know that he, too, would one day be sitting on his pony just like Slow was doing now, ready for his first hunt.

After some time, Slow and the other hunters reached the top of a steep hill and saw below them a vast herd of buffalo grazing in the tall grass. Slow could

> But Slow knew that accompanying the warriors on a buffalo hunt was the true first step to becoming a Sioux warrior.

feel his heart pounding as they waited for the leaders of the hunt to give the signal to charge, then they all raced down the hill toward the still-unaware herd.

All of the training Slow had received from his father and the other men of the tribe was now more than just a lesson. It was real, and one can easily imagine the action of his first hunt. Slow dug his knees into the sides of his pony and rode fearlessly into the center of the herd. Right away, Slow spotted a bull calf. Quickly, he raced toward the animal, holding on tightly to his pony with his legs and using one hand to take an arrow out of his quiver and the other hand to put it in his bow. Confused, the bull calf started toward his mother, but Slow circled the animal, cutting off its

Young Sioux boys dreamed about going on their first buffalo hunt—one of the most important steps toward manhood. Sitting Bull's experience would have been much like the scene in this 19th-century hand-colored engraving.

attempt to escape. Now, Slow took aim and shot the arrow. It struck, and the calf looked up in surprise. Immediately, Slow shot another arrow. The animal staggered a few steps, then fell to the ground. Slow gave a shout of victory.

One of Slow's uncles had seen what had happened and rode over to congratulate his nephew. Then he helped Slow cut up the calf, so it could be carried back to camp. The Sioux only killed as many buffalo as they thought they would need to feed the members of the tribe before the next hunt. A piece of the meat about the size of a man's head was always left on the ground as an offering to *Wakan Tanka*, in gratitude for the gift of the buffalo.

## A Generous Son

In Sioux tradition, a boy was taught humility by giving away at least a portion of his first buffalo kill. Slow decided to offer *all* of his buffalo meat to poorer members of the tribe who didn't have sons who were warriors, so they could have extra portions at several meals. Slow's family was filled with pride at his generosity. Everyone told Sitting Bull and Her-Holy-Door that their son was special, and Slow could see the pride in their eyes. Where some boys his age might have been content to **rest on their laurels** or to become arrogant, it only made Slow want to do even more for his tribe. Later in life, Slow, who was by then known as Sitting Bull, would tell people, "When I was ten years old I was famous as a hunter. My specialty was buffalo calves. I gave the [ones] I killed to the poor who had no horses. I was considered a good man . . . For four years after I was ten years old, I killed buffalo and fed [my father's] people, and thus [I] became one of the fathers of the tribe."

Over the next year, Slow was allowed to take part in tribal rituals alongside the other men. He danced with them, and he sat with them as the elders told stories only for the ears of the men. While they still passed down tales about ancient warriors, they now included ones about people with lighter skin. Tribes to the south told how these light-skinned people were beginning to move onto their lands and to take their food, which *Wakan Tanka* had provided for their people since the beginning of time.

Slow was fascinated by what he was hearing. He couldn't imagine people with skin as white as the clouds in the sky. He was interested in their strange ways and wondered if they would ever travel north to where the Hunkpapa lived.

As Sitting Bull neared manhood, more and more white settlers were pouring onto sacred Sioux land. This 1889 photograph shows homesteaders setting up camp near Indian Territory in what is now Oklahoma.

# CHAPTER 3

# His Name Is Now Sitting Bull

*I kill only game—the beasts that we need for food.*

By the time Slow was fourteen years old, in 1845, he had already killed many buffalo and was considered to be one of the best hunters of the tribe. But he still had not been on a raid against other tribes. Slow decided that it was time to take this next step into manhood. But who would he be fighting? The Assiniboine and the Crow were mortal enemies of the Sioux, but the Sioux also did battle from time to time with the Cree and the Northern Blackfeet.

Although Slow was still *slow* in many of the things he did, he was very skillful in the things that counted for Hunkpapa warriors. He could shoot several arrows in succession while riding his pony at full speed across the plains. He was also good at positioning his body along one side of his galloping pony, so that the animal would act as a shield between him and anyone he was fighting. Even though Slow wasn't as tall as some of the other boys his age, he was strong and muscular, and he knew in his heart that he was ready to fight.

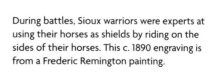

During battles, Sioux warriors were experts at using their horses as shields by riding on the sides of their horses. This c. 1890 engraving is from a Frederic Remington painting.

# The Plains Indians

Native Americans who lived on the vast expanse of the rolling hills and plains in the center of the United States (and north into Canada) were known as the Plains Indians. Their dominance of the region lasted from 1750 until 1890. The Plains Indians can be divided into two broad groups that overlap some. The first group was **nomadic** and followed the great herds of buffalo. In addition to the tribes of the Great Sioux Nation, this group included the Arapaho, Assiniboine, Cheyenne, Comanche, Crow, Gros Ventre, Kiowa, Northern Blackfeet, Kiowa Apache, and Sarsi. The second group, sometimes called the Prairie Indians, lived in permanent villages and raised crops in addition to hunting for buffalo. These tribes included the Arikara, Iowa, Kansa, Mandan, Omaha, Osage, Oto, Pawnee, Ponca, Wichita, Hidatsa, Missouri, Quapaw, and Caddo.

Nomadic Plains Indians, as seen in this photograph (left) of three Sioux warriors from the late 1800s, constantly moved across the Great Plains. Prairie Indians such as the Mandan lived in permanent villages, in huts like the one shown in this 1844 painting (right).

# A New Weapon

When Slow learned that a war party would be heading out to fight soon, he made the decision to go with them.

After the warriors had left, he waited for a time, until he felt they would be far enough from the camp that they wouldn't send him back once they discovered he had joined them. Even though he knew he wasn't really old enough to be part of a raid, he slung the quiver containing his bow and arrows over his shoulder and urged his pony in the direction of the war party.

Riding hard and fast, Slow soon came within sight of the men. When the warriors riding at the rear of the party saw him, they seemed surprised, but didn't say anything—probably because they respected the bravery Slow was displaying by joining them. Slow was counting on his father respecting his bravery, too. Upon seeing his son, Sitting Bull's proud look didn't disappoint the young warrior. On the contrary, he told Slow that he must perform a brave act.

Sitting Bull gave his son a long cane-like weapon called a *coup stick*. It was decorated with holy images that the Sioux believed would help them in battle. To a Sioux warrior, the practice called *counting coup* showed how brave a warrior was. The custom called for a warrior to ride right up to the enemy and strike him with the stick. It brought the greatest honor to the Sioux warrior—even more than downing an

To a Sioux warrior, the practice of counting coup showed how brave he was. This 1910 photograph shows a feathered coup stick much like the one Sitting Bull would have used to knock an enemy from his horse.

enemy warrior with an arrow, which could be accomplished from a safe distance away. Using a coup stick required a warrior to get close to the enemy, so he could knock him off his horse. Once the enemy had fallen, other Sioux warriors could also count coup, but their coups would not be as great as the Sioux warrior who had first struck the enemy.

Slow knew that Hunkpapa warriors were judged by the number of coups they counted—that is, the number of warriors they had struck with the coup stick and knocked from their horses. Anyone in the tribe could tell that number by how many feathers the warrior wore in his hair.

Slow was now a member of the war party. As they rode off in the direction of the Missouri River, searching the horizons for signs of their enemies, Slow could hardly wait to show his bravery, not only for the glory it would bring him, but for the honor it would bring to his family.

## Counting Coup

Suddenly the party's forward scout gave them a signal that a band of Crow warriors was headed their way. The Hunkpapa quickly dismounted and hid behind a small hill. As the men waited for the Crow to get closer, Slow looked around, still amazed that he was about to fight in a real battle, not in the game battles he had played with his friends. Like the other men, he was dressed only in a loincloth with beads strung around his body, standing next to his red-painted horse.

Finally, Slow could stand it no longer. Without thinking about the consequences, he jumped onto his pony, dug his heels into the animal's flanks to spur him on, and charged toward the Crow by himself. Surprised by Slow's bold action, the rest of the war party followed the teenage warrior and raced toward the approaching Crow. They weren't about to let a young boy take all their glory.

Leading the Sioux war party, Slow could see that the Crow warriors had been taken by surprise. The Crow reined in their horses and stared at the approaching Sioux youth. Then, realizing the danger, the Crow warriors quickly turned and started racing back in the direction they had come from. Within minutes, most of the Crow warriors had disappeared from view, but a few who had fallen behind suddenly panicked and leaped off their horses. Immediately, the one closest to Slow put an arrow in his bow and aimed it at the fast-approaching young warrior.

*. . . Slow looked around, still amazed that he was about to fight in a real battle . . .*

All of a sudden, Slow forgot everything that he had been taught. Instead of dropping to one side of his pony so it would act as a shield between him and the Crow's arrow, Slow sat erect on the animal and continued to race toward the enemy warrior. But before the Crow could let his arrow fly, Slow was beside him in an instant and used his coup stick to knock the man down. When Slow turned his pony around, he saw the man lying on the ground, writhing in pain from the blow. The victorious youth shouted in triumph as he watched other Hunkpapa warriors attack the man with their weapons and put him out of his misery.

Within the next few minutes, the Hunkpapa, Slow among them, had either killed or chased away the few remaining Crow warriors and had captured several of their horses. When the battle was over, Slow could hardly contain his pride and joy. He had counted coup, and now he belonged to the elite members of the tribe.

# A New Name

As the Hunkpapa war party headed back to their camp, Slow rode alongside his father, who told him again and again how brave his actions had been and how he had honored his family. When the war party finally arrived back at the camp, all the warriors rode around proudly, whooping and shouting about their victory over the enemy Crow. Slow's voice was undoubtedly the loudest heard by the women, children, and old men who greeted them.

Later that evening, Sitting Bull covered Slow's whole body in black paint, a sign of victory, then helped him onto a large stallion. As the people cheered, Sitting Bull led his son around the camp. He told the tribe that because of what Slow had done in battle, the young boy deserved a new name. In an act of ultimate tribute, Sitting Bull bestowed his own name on his son. Slow would now be known as Sitting Bull. His father took the name Jumping Bull. Everyone in the tribe agreed that Sitting Bull was worthy of his new name, and that he would surely accomplish many great things in his lifetime.

After a successful battle, Sioux war parties would return home, whooping and shouting about their victory—usually over the Crow.

# CHAPTER 4

# A Message from Wakan Tanka

*I am satisfied that I was brought into this life for a purpose; otherwise, why am I here?*

The Hunkpapa were fierce warriors. They usually showed no mercy to their enemies, especially the Crow and the Assiniboine. Once an enemy had been struck down with either arrows or knives, the Hunkpapa warrior proceeded to remove the dead man's scalp. These victory scalps were highly prized by many Native American tribes because they believed that a person's soul was located in the hair.

Often, the triumphant warrior would hang the scalps from his horse for everyone to see how many "enemy souls" he possessed.

Yet, there was another side to the Hunkpapa: They were a people who loved and respected the land and the animals living on it. After all,

When a Native American scalped an enemy, as shown in this color print called *The Death Cry* from the late 1800s, he believed that he now possessed that person's soul.

it was what allowed the tribe to survive. For this, the Hunkpapa gave thanks to *Wakan Tanka*, whom they believed controlled everything in their lives.

*Wakan Tanka* often spoke to the Sioux through birds, deer, or buffalo—wild creatures that the Sioux believed had special powers. Not every member of the tribe could understand these voices, though. It had to be someone whom *Wakan Tanka* had endowed with this power. In Sitting Bull's band, Jumping Bull had this gift. Soon after Sitting Bull received his new name, he realized that he, too, could understand what the animals were saying.

## Grizzly Bear Vision

While out hunting by himself one day, Sitting Bull grew tired and lay down to rest in the shade of a tree. Within minutes, he was asleep and dreaming that a huge grizzly bear was chasing him through the woods, across the creeks and rivers, and up and down the hills. Suddenly, Sitting Bull awakened with a start. He was shivering uncontrollably and had broken out in a cold sweat. Sitting Bull immediately sat up and looked around, wanting to make sure that it had indeed been a dream and that there truly was not a bear nearby, ready to pounce on him. Normally, a Hunkpapa would not fear anything, but grizzly bears were especially dangerous. Their fur and skin were so thick that arrows more often than not bounced off the fierce animal.

Sitting Bull felt so unsettled by the experience that he decided to go back to the camp. Just as he started to stand up, he heard a woodpecker pecking against the side of a tree. Right away, Sitting Bull recognized the pecking as a message from *Wakan Tanka*. Sitting Bull listened carefully. The woodpecker told him to sit

# Grizzly Bears

The grizzly bear's habitat extends from Alaska, south through much of western Canada, and into the American states of Idaho, Montana, Washington, and Wyoming. The male grizzly sometimes reaches a height of eight feet and can weigh up to nine hundred pounds. Native Americans held the grizzly in awe and treated it with great respect. Many tribes thought of them as gods. They were astounded at how strong the animals were and at how quickly they could move in spite of their size. Grizzly bears became important figures in many Native American legends. Because the grizzly bear was seen as an object of power and strength, its image is often found in many Native American paintings and engraved on Native American jewelry.

Because of their power and strength, grizzly bears, such as the one pictured here, were revered by Native Americans.

back down under the tree. Something important was about to happen. Sitting Bull did as *Wakan Tanka* asked.

Almost immediately, a huge grizzly bear came out of the woods, lumbering directly toward Sitting Bull. What he had dreamed was now coming true. His instincts told him to jump up and run back to camp, but that would be disobeying *Wakan Tanka*. So Sitting Bull closed his eyes and remained as still as he could, barely allowing himself to breathe.

Sitting Bull could feel the grizzly coming closer and closer, but he willed himself not to move. He heard the huge bear's breathing and knew the animal was only inches from his face. Sitting Bull prepared to die.

All at once, the grizzly grunted, and then Sitting Bull

*Right away, Sitting Bull recognized the pecking as a message from* Wakan Tanka.

could no longer feel his hot breath. He opened his eyes just wide enough to see the bear heading back toward the forest. Sitting Bull stayed where he was for several more minutes, just in case the bear decided to return. Then he stood up on wobbly legs and looked up into the branches of the tree. The woodpecker was still there, and Sitting Bull thanked it for telling him to stay put under the tree. He was sure his life had been saved for a greater purpose—to devote the rest of it to helping his people.

Now, Sitting Bull knew that *Wakan Tanka* considered him special. He was brave. He could talk to the animals and the birds. Still, Sitting Bull knew that the greatest Hunkpapa only reached purity in mind and body through visions they received *directly* from *Wakan Tanka*. Thus, in 1846, when Sitting Bull turned fifteen, he let it be known to his father that he was ready for this next step into manhood—the *vision quest*, where he would find out what the future held for him.

## Native American Myths

Among all Native American tribes, there is a very strong belief that everything in their world—every human, every animal, and every tree and grain of sand in nature—is embodied by a spiritual power from a single life force called the *Great Mystery*. As a part of this spiritual outlook, Native Americans believe that, in times of trouble, animals will come to them and tell them how to deal with these difficult situations. Sitting Bull was often visited by different animals that told him how to prepare for events in his future.

## Visiting the Shaman

The spiritual leader of the Hunkpapa was called a *shaman*, and one day Jumping Bull took Sitting Bull to meet the tribe's shaman. But Sitting Bull was a bit anxious. He had heard stories about other young men who had asked the shaman about their vision quests, only to be told *Wakan Tanka* wasn't listening to them. At that point, the boys knew they would never be great warriors and would always have to follow others whom *Wakan Tanka* had chosen. Still, Sitting Bull knew he must proceed. In his heart, he truly believed that *Wakan Tanka* would speak to him of his greatness.

After Jumping Bull spoke with the shaman, the holy man agreed to help Sitting Bull with his vision quest. Like others before him, Sitting Bull began preparing himself to go through the difficult ritual: He probably remained with the shaman for almost a month, all the while listening to the spiritual leader tell him the history of the Sioux. Sitting Bull had heard some of the stories before, but the shaman's version had more depth and seemed more real.

One morning, Sitting Bull awakened to find the shaman dressed in his buffalo robes, standing over him. He told Sitting Bull to get up, to dress only in a loincloth, and to follow him up into the nearby hills. Without a word and with his heart pounding, Sitting Bull did as he was told. Near the summit of a hill, Sitting Bull saw a dome-shaped hut, called a *sweat lodge*. It was made from willow poles and covered with buffalo skins to make it airtight. The entrance faced east, toward the rising sun, which the shaman said symbolized Sitting Bull's rebirth as a true Hunkpapa warrior.

This photograph from the early 1900s shows Saliva, an Oglala Sioux shaman. A shaman helped Sitting Bull to achieve his vision quest.

The shaman went to work and built a fire outside the hut. He then placed several large stones on the flames. Moving inside the lodge, the holy man dug a deep hole in the center of it. He filled the hole with herbs he had carried in a pouch. Finally, the shaman moved the heated rocks into the hole, on top of the herbs, and poured water on them. The lodge immediately filled with a fragrant steam cloud. Sitting Bull was told to sit at the edge of the hole, and he obeyed. Soon, Sitting Bull began to feel as though his skin were on fire. Sweat poured from his body. Just when Sitting Bull thought he couldn't stand it any longer, the shaman told him to leave the lodge, to go down to the nearby creek, and to jump into the freezing water.

Sitting Bull waited inside a sweat lodge—much like the Cheyenne sweat lodge whose frame is shown in this 1910 photograph—to learn from *Wakan Tanka* what the future held for him.

Again, Sitting Bull did as he was told and gasped at the icy shock to his body. When he climbed out of the creek and returned to the lodge, the shaman told him he was leaving. He instructed Sitting Bull to go back into the lodge, naked, and wait until *Wakan Tanka* had decided whether the young warrior would be visited by a vision or not.

For Sitting Bull, it became more and more difficult to ignore his shivering body and the gnawing hunger in his belly. The first night came and went, and by the second night, the anxious warrior was almost ready to admit that *Wakan Tanka* was not looking kindly upon him—the reasons for which he could not understand. Had he done anything to anger the Great Spirit?

## In the Presence of the Great Spirit

Finally, by the third day, Sitting Bull no longer craved either water or food, and he felt himself floating free of his body. When he looked up, he saw clouds in the sky. As he continued to gaze in wonderment, the clouds parted, and Sitting Bull saw a bright light and heard a voice inside him saying he was now in the presence of the Great Spirit.

After a time—Sitting Bull wasn't sure how long—the light faded and the clouds came together again. The teenager was once again sitting alone. He stood up and made his way down the hill, back to his village, and to the shaman's tepee. After describing to the shaman what had happened, the holy man told him what the vision meant: Sitting Bull would become a great leader of the Sioux.

# CHAPTER 5

# Becoming a Leader

*I tell you the truth; since I was raised I have done nothing bad.*

In 1851, when he was twenty, Sitting Bull married a young woman named Light Hair, who soon died giving birth to a son. Four years later, Sitting Bull's son took ill and died. Sitting Bull had now lost his wife and child. But as was the Sioux tradition, Sitting Bull would marry again—several times, as a matter of fact—during his life. His second wife was Snow-on-Her, and his third was Scarlet Woman. There were two other wives as well, whose names are lost in history.

In 1852, Sitting Bull was chosen to be a member of the Strong Hearts, a group of men considered to be the best warriors. It was from this group that chiefs were often chosen, and it was unusual that they allowed someone so young to join them. But Sitting Bull was very special, and everyone knew it. Sitting Bull made such a good impression on the other members of the Strong Hearts that he was chosen to be a sash-wearer. As such, he wore a headdress decorated with many crow feathers, two buffalo horns, and a long streamer made from fur. The long sash he wore was also decorated with feathers and dragged on the ground. As a sash-wearer, Sitting Bull was expected during battles with enemy warriors to drive a lance through the end of the sash, fastening himself to the earth. This told the men he was fighting that he would choose death before he would run away from a battle. Sitting Bull could not have been more proud of the honor.

## Ritual of the Sun Dance

The Sun Dance was the most important religious ceremony that Sioux warriors repeated each year. Through the dance, the Sioux showed *Wakan Tanka* that they were willing to suffer great pain in order to demonstrate their gratitude for all the things he did for the tribe. The Sun Dance always took place in the month of June. By then, both the days and nights were warm on the northern Great Plains. It would now be easier than in harsh winter months to follow wherever *Wakan Tanka's* spiritual guidance took them.

In preparation, Sitting Bull, now in his mid-twenties, listened carefully to the instructions given to him not only by the shaman but by the men whom he would be joining. By tradition, no women danced in this ceremony.

To prepare for the dance, a large circle was set up in the middle of the Hunkpapa's camp. A special forked cottonwood tree was chopped down for a pole and painted yellow, red, blue, and green, with paint made from berries and different colored minerals in the area. With **rawhide** ropes attached to it, the pole was then set up in the center of the circle.

On the day of the Sun Dance, the shaman called Sitting Bull to a cottonwood tree where he sat while they painted his hands and feet red and his shoulders blue. Sitting Bull then lay down on a bed of fresh herbs, located near the center pole. Using a sharp knife, the shaman made cuts into Sitting Bull's chest and back. He then inserted long wooden pins, fastening them to the strips of skin between the slashes. Sitting Bull wanted to cry out from the pain, but knew it would disgrace his family. According to

Sioux tradition, women in the tribe cried for him. When Sitting Bull bled, the women standing nearest to him used soft grass to wipe the blood away.

Once the skewers had been attached to Sitting Bull's skin, he along with the other dancers—often, there were up to four warriors participating—got up, and the skewers were fastened to the leather straps on the cottonwood pole. Then the dancing began: The men

*Sitting Bull wanted to cry out from the pain, but knew it would disgrace his family.*

leaned away from the pole, keeping the ropes taut as they pulled on the skewers. The Sun Dance continued until each warrior fell to the ground from exhaustion, causing the skewers to tear away from the skin. One by one, the warriors' wounds were dressed with buffalo fat by the women who had been watching the dance. For Sitting Bull as well as the others, there would be deep scars where the skewers had been torn away, but it made him proud that he could now take his place as a man among the other men of the tribe.

The Sun Dance was the most important religious ceremony for the Sioux. As seen in this photograph from the early 1900s, a rawhide rope was attached on one end to a wooden pole and on the other end to skewers under strips of skin on the dancer's chest (or sometimes on the dancer's back).

# Stealing Horses

In 1856, Sitting Bull and the men in his tribe needed some new horses to replace some that had been gored to death during buffalo hunts and others that were getting too old to ride in battle. As was the custom, they planned to steal these horses from the Crow tribe. A raiding party of over one hundred men was formed, and the Hunkpapa set out for the Yellowstone River. They all carried their traditional weapons, but some of them, including Sitting Bull, also had new **muzzle-loading guns**, which they had bought from traders.

When the warriors finally came upon a Crow camp, they waited until the Crow were asleep. They then entered the camp and quietly began leading the Crow horses away. Although the Hunkpapa were experts at entering and leaving enemy campsites

By the mid-1850s, Sioux warriors fought battles not only with their traditional bows and arrows but also with muzzle-loading guns—similar to the ones in this photograph—that they bought from white traders.

# Native American Weapons

The weapons of Native Americans were adapted to each tribe's fighting style. Some used bows and arrows with pointed tips made out of chipped stone. There were spears made with stone points as well as those made of chipped bone and antlers. Other throwing weapons included knives and lances. For protection, shields made of buffalo hide were used. Later, many warriors used guns, which they received from white settlers.

But the most well-known Native American weapon was probably the tomahawk. Not just a weapon, a tomahawk was also a tool that was used to chop down trees. When turned to the flat side, it could be used to hammer wooden stakes into the ground. The first Native American tomahawks had wood handles and stone, usually flint, blades. Because tomahawks were such powerful weapons, though, the United States military began to use them, too, fashioning the blades out of metal. In fact, tomahawks were even used during the Vietnam War in the 1960s and '70s.

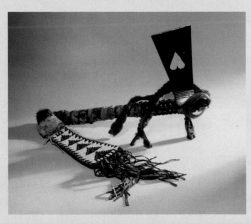

Native Americans used the tomahawk, such as the one pictured here, both for battles and for daily chores.

without a sound, this time some of the sleeping Crow sensed danger and woke up. Within minutes, they ran to the corral to check on their horses and knew immediately what was happening. Gathering their weapons, the Crow jumped onto the few remaining horses and took off after the Hunkpapa.

Sitting Bull and the other men could hear the whoops of the Crow as they headed toward them. Because of the stolen horses, the Hunkpapa just couldn't travel as fast. Thinking quickly, they decided to send some of the younger warriors back to their camp with the animals, while Sitting Bull and the older warriors remained to fight the Crow. They took their positions behind whatever cover they could find. Just after sunrise, the Hunkpapa saw the approaching Crow. When the chasing Crow finally rode by, Sitting Bull and the other warriors bombarded them with their muzzle-loaders.

Two of the Crow were killed immediately, but the others managed to jump from their horses and run for cover. Over the next few minutes, both sides exchanged volleys of arrows and muzzle shots. During the fierce fighting, one of the younger Hunkpapa warriors was killed

*. . . Sitting Bull and the other warriors bombarded them with their muzzle-loaders.*

by a Crow arrow. After a while, when neither side seemed to be gaining any ground in the battle, Sitting Bull decided to get closer to the enemy. He ran forward, toward two Crow who were hidden. Kneeling down on one knee, Sitting Bull aimed his muzzle-loader at one of the men. But the Crow also had a muzzle-loader, and fired first at Sitting Bull. One of the muzzle balls, about the size of a small rock, smashed through Sitting Bull's shield and entered his left foot. Sitting Bull ignored the pain and calmly fired at the Crow, wounding him. Sitting Bull finished

# Horses

Before the arrival of Europeans, horses were not a part of Native American culture. But around 1540, Spanish explorers introduced the beasts to a few tribes who were living in the southwest (what is present-day western Texas, New Mexico, and Arizona). These tribes, however, found little use for the animals and preferred using dogs to pull their travois when moving their belongings from camp to camp.

About two hundred years later, the Plains Indians, such as the Sioux, realized that horses could change their way of life. Because the buffalo herds moved great distances during the seasons, it had always been difficult for Native Americans to follow them. Now, with horses, the hunters could outrun the buffalo, giving them an enormous advantage. Riding fast and powerful horses also allowed warriors of one tribe to attack enemy camps at night and quickly get away.

Spanish explorers introduced horses to the Native Americans of the Great Plains. This 1898 illustration by Frederic Remington shows Spanish explorer Francisco Coronado in the American Southwest in 1540.

killing the Crow with a knife and then took his scalp. The other Crow warrior retreated. The Hunkpapa were now free to return to camp.

When Sitting Bull and the war party returned to their camp, they mourned the dead Hunkpapa warrior, Paints Brown, for four days, and then they asked permission from his relatives to hold a victory dance. This was granted, and they celebrated their victory over the Crow by parading the captured horses around the grounds so everyone could see how magnificent the animals were. Sitting Bull was the hero of the battle, the tribe was told, because he was the one who caused the Crow to flee. Although his foot wound caused him great pain, Sitting Bull still basked in the glory of the victory and of the praise from the other warriors.

While Sitting Bull's wound eventually healed, it didn't heal perfectly, and he would always walk with a limp. He would tell people, "[It] took [a] long time to kill these people. Here is where I got wounded in [the] leg and got off of [my] horse and killed this man. [There were] no prisoners in that fight."

## Assiniboine Brother

Although Sitting Bull was known as a fierce warrior, he was also thought of as a kind and gentle man, and that side of him became even more evident in the winter of 1857, when he was twenty-six years old.

During a Hunkpapa raid on an Assiniboine camp, an entire family was killed—all except an eleven-year-old boy. When Sitting Bull rode up to the family's tepee, he was certain that the other Hunkpapa warriors were going to kill the youth, too. After all, the Assiniboine had always been the enemies of the Hunkpapa. Sitting Bull saw the boy looking at him, and in that moment, the brave warrior saw something extraordinary—perhaps a courageous spirit—in the youth's stare that touched his heart. Just as one of the Hunkpapa warriors aimed an arrow at the boy's chest, the youth shouted, "Big brother!" to Sitting Bull. No one knows why. Perhaps he felt a connection to Sitting Bull as well, or perhaps he was just trying to save his own life.

Whatever the reason, Sitting Bull shouted to his men not to shoot. He thought the lad was too brave to die, and told his fellow warriors he would take the boy and make him his brother. The other Hunkpapa argued with Sitting Bull that the young one should die, but Sitting Bull remained firm in his decision. The youth accompanied the war party back to their camp, where Sitting Bull named him Stays-

*Although Sitting Bull was known as a fierce warrior, he was also thought of as a kind and gentle man . . .*

Back. It wasn't long before everyone realized that Sitting Bull had done the right thing. Stays-Back remained loyal to Sitting Bull for the rest of his life.

## The Death of Jumping Bull

In the spring of 1859, tragedy struck Sitting Bull and his family. After a successful buffalo hunt, the Hunkpapa were attacked while traveling to another camp by a band of about fifty Crow warriors. Sitting Bull took off after some of the Crow warriors across the plains, but Jumping Bull stayed with the main band to fight the remaining Crow. After the two enemies traded arrows and gunfire for a while, most of the Crow began a slow retreat, but one Crow warrior with a gun stood his ground, which intimidated some of the Hunkpapa. Jumping Bull saw this as an act of cowardice. He told the Hunkpapa that he would fight the enemy alone—even though he was now an old man.

Unfortunately, Jumping Bull's bow and arrows were no match for the rifle of the Crow, and he was wounded. Still, he wouldn't give up. He dashed after the Crow warrior with his knife. But the Crow jumped off his horse, and, brandishing his own knife, stabbed Jumping Bull repeatedly with it. The old warrior lay dead on the ground.

*In the spring of 1859, tragedy struck Sitting Bull and his family.*

At that moment, Sitting Bull returned to the camp and saw what had happened to his father. Seething with anger and full of disbelief, he dug his heels into the flanks of his horse and raced toward the fleeing Crow warrior. When Sitting Bull reached the Crow, he thrust his lance through the man, killing him instantly.

Sitting Bull and his family, along with the rest of the tribe, went into mourning. As was the custom, some painted their faces black and some cried for days. Everyone knew what a loss Jumping Bull's death was to the Hunkpapa. Still, Sitting Bull took solace in the knowledge that, in the tradition of his tribe, he had avenged his father's death: He had killed the Crow warrior who had slaughtered his father.

# CHAPTER 6

# The Movement West

*I do not understand why the white man leaves his own land to invade ours.*

By the mid-1800s white settlers were moving west in droves. Many felt they were destined by God to expand the country's borders all over the North American continent and to control and populate the land as they saw fit. For these settlers, this belief, called *Manifest Destiny*, justified their western expansion. It was a way, everyone believed, to spread America's **democracy**. For all the positive aspects of Manifest Destiny, though, there was also a dark side. In the name of this doctrine, Americans took whatever land they wanted, wherever they found it, settling, planting, and farming it.

To the horror of many Native American tribes, these new arrivals began taking more and more of what the Indians considered their land—land they believed had been given to them in trust by *Wakan Tanka*. When conflicts arose between the United States government and

A woman representing "Manifest Destiny" is shown leading settlers across the continent in this 1872 painting by John Gast titled *American Progress.*

Native Americans over ownership, the Native Americans almost always lost the battle. Many of them were forced to live on what were called reservations—land that for the most part was unproductive and bare of game. It was a move that would almost certainly destroy their cultures.

## Fighting the "Bluecoats"

One group affected early on by the westward movement was another branch of the Sioux called the Dakota. Living in the state of Minnesota, the Dakota had lost their land and had almost been driven to starvation. When the Dakota finally decided to fight, they ended up killing several hundred white people, and the governor of the state sent U.S. Army troops, led by Colonel Henry H. Sibley, to force them back onto the reservation.

At that time, the Hunkpapa as well as other Plains Indians did not yet feel the encroachment that the Dakota were experiencing. The United States was embroiled in a civil war and the U.S. Army was preoccupied by it. These Plains Indians could still hunt their buffalo and live their lives as they had always done.

But a drought on the Great Plains caused Sitting Bull and his band of Hunkpapa to move where water was more available and the buffalo more abundant. When Sitting Bull and his people crossed the Missouri River, they met some of the Dakota who were warring with Colonel Sibley's "bluecoats"—the name Native Americans used for **cavalry** troops because of the color of their uniforms. At the Dakota's request, Sitting Bull's band joined in the fighting, because he knew that if the Dakota lost this struggle, the Hunkpapa could be next.

*It was a move that would almost certainly destroy their cultures.*

Colonel Henry H. Sibley, shown here in this mid-1800s photograph, led the American troops that forced the Dakota back onto their reservation.

Although the combined Indian forces distinguished themselves at two battles—later called the Battle of Dead Buffalo Lake and the Battle of Stony Lake—the Army guns were just too powerful for them. Fearing if they continued the fight, they would eventually lose many more men, the Indians decided to retreat back across to the west side of the Missouri River. Still, Sitting Bull felt they had stood up as well as they could to the superior American troops.

## More Conflicts

Over the next year, with the American Civil War winding
down, tensions between the Indians of the Great Plains and the
white settlers and soldiers began to increase. In 1864, Colonel
J. M. Chivington and his soldiers came upon a friendly Cheyenne
village near Fort Lyon, Colorado. Learning that the men were
away hunting, the soldiers massacred the women and children,
for no other reason than to get rid of some Indians. A few months
later, some of the Cheyenne warriors who had lost their entire
families traveled north to where Sitting Bull's band was camped.
They told them what had happened and that they planned to
declare war on the white settlers. The Cheyenne wanted the
Hunkpapa to join them. When the Cheyenne leader offered
Sitting Bull a peace pipe, the Sioux leader took it and smoked
it, signaling that the Hunkpapa would now fight the settlers, too.
Sitting Bull realized that this was a struggle for the very existence
of all Native American tribes.

As shown in this hand-colored woodcut from the late 1800s, soldiers led by Colonel
J. M. Chivington massacred all the women and children at a Cheyenne village on Sand
Creek, near Fort Lyon, Colorado, in 1864.

# The American Civil War

Between 1861 and 1865, civil war between the North and the South ravaged the United States. The war was fought mostly over the question of slavery. Whereas the South depended on the slavery system for its economic survival, the North did not and called for it to end. When Abraham Lincoln was elected president in 1860, his Republican party wanted to limit slavery to the states that already had it. Afraid of being outnumbered by the non-slave states, eleven southern states formed the Confederate States of America and **seceded** from the United States. War broke out in 1861 after the United States refused to recognize this secession. Although the Confederate army, under General Robert E. Lee, won the First Battle of Bull Run in 1861, the superior power of the North soon turned the tide with a victory at Gettysburg in July 1863, five months after Lincoln had proclaimed that all slaves in the Confederate states were free. General Lee finally surrendered in April 1865. Over 618,000 Americans lost their lives.

As shown in this late 1800s lithograph, Union forces defeated Confederate forces at the Battle of Gettysburg on July 3, 1863. This battle marked a turning point in the American Civil War.

Following the end of the Civil War, the white settlers continued their march westward. Soon, all the different tribes of the Great Sioux Nation began to worry about the endless flow of white settlers onto their lands. The different chiefs of the bands decided that the time had come for them to join together, as one force, and under one chief, to stop this migration. The tribes of the Great Sioux Nation decided that this great new chief should be selected during the time of the Sun Dance. The Hunkpapa, the Oglala, the Miniconjou, the Sans Arc, the Yanktonai, the Two Kettle, and the Blackfeet would all be there. Also joining them would be the Cheyenne and the Arapaho, who were not Sioux, but who wanted to unite with the Sioux against the white settlers.

## The Great Chief

In the summer of 1869, Sitting Bull was the unanimous choice of all of the other chiefs in attendance. They determined that of all the Sioux warriors, Sitting Bull was the one who was most favored by *Wakan Tanka*. The entire gathering agreed with the chiefs: Sitting Bull was the most worthy to be the chief of the united tribes.

After Sitting Bull had been chosen, the chiefs ordered that a lodge be built to hold a special ceremony to honor the great chief in his new role. When it was completed, the chiefs spread a buffalo hide on the ground. Sitting Bull sat on it, and they carried him to the lodge. Inside, they smoked a peace pipe, and as they smoked it, they prayed to *Wakan Tanka*. They told Sitting Bull that all of them, along with their warriors, would always follow him into battle. The chiefs then gave him a new gun, a new bow with arrows, and a new war bonnet, or feathered headdress.

This 1885 photograph of Sitting Bull, taken by D. F. Barry in Bismarck, Dakota Territory, is one of the most famous images of the great chief.

Crazy Horse, a member of the Oglala tribe, was named Sitting Bull's second in command. To end the ceremony, the chiefs presented Sitting Bull with a white horse. He mounted the horse, and the chiefs led him around the camp, so all could see their new leader—the one who would stop the white settlers from taking the rest of their land.

# CHAPTER 7

# The Black Robe

*Tell the Black Robe we shall meet him and his friends with arms stretched out, ready to embrace him.*

Once again, all of the Great Plains Indians, including the united Great Sioux Nation, fought violent and very bloody battles with the white settlers and the soldiers of the U.S. Army. Both groups seemed ready to continue the struggle until every living being on one side or the other was dead. Finally, a Catholic priest named Father Pierre-Jean De Smet was sent by the U.S. government—most notably, by the Office of Indian Affairs—to meet with the Indians in hopes of putting an end to the bloodshed.

Along with an interpreter, Father Jean, as he was simply called, traveled the countryside in a carriage that was decorated with a black cross. On the day they neared Sitting Bull's camp on the Powder River, lookouts ran back to tell Sitting Bull that a "black robe" (their name for Catholic priests) was headed their way. As a tireless missionary, Father Jean was considered a man of unquestioned integrity. He had ministered and cared for Native Americans and had gained their trust. He was able to travel to areas where almost no other white man could enter safely—a fact recognized by government officials and the U.S. Army. Sitting Bull told the lookouts to tell the priest that he would not only receive the "black robe,"

## Bureau of Indian Affairs

As far back as 1775, there have been Indian agencies that were created by the Second Continental Congress. It was their responsibility to negotiate treaties with Native Americans and to obtain their **neutrality** during the American Revolutionary War. In 1824, during the era of westward expansion, the Office of Indian Affairs was formed. It was renamed the Bureau of Indian Affairs in 1947. As a federal agency of the Department of the Interior, the Bureau of Indian Affairs has the responsibility of administering more than 103,000 square miles of land held in trust by the United States for all Native American tribes. It also provides schools on reservations for almost fifty thousand Native American children.

but he would listen to what he had to say as well. He gave his assurance that no harm would come to him.

## Father Jean's Message

Father Jean reached Sitting Bull's camp on June 19. He had never before seen so many Indians gathered in one place. The camp was home to several thousand people from all the tribes making up the united Great Sioux Nation. Father Jean was both astonished and greatly moved when the Indians began singing as they followed his carriage toward Sitting Bull's tepee, where the great chief greeted them. He invited the priest and interpreter inside, where he offered them food.

Father Jean told Sitting Bull that the U.S. government was ready to live in peace with all the Indian tribes. In response,

Sitting Bull said, "Black-robe, . . . [the] whites provoked the war; their injustices, their indignities to our families, the cruel, unheard-of, and wholly unprovoked massacre . . . shook all the veins which bind and support me. . . . Today thou art amongst us, and in thy presence my arms stretch to the ground as if dead. I will listen to thy good words." The great chief agreed to go to Fort Rice, which was located in North Dakota, to meet with government representatives there. In an effort to influence the direction of the meeting before it even started, Sitting Bull emphasized that under no circumstances would the Great Sioux Nation agree to give away any of its land. He also insisted that all the soldiers had to leave their forts.

Major Charles A. R. Dimon, commander of Fort Rice in Dakota Territory, is shown in this 1865 photograph with some of the chiefs from tribes in the area. It was at Fort Rice where the Treaty of 1868 was signed.

# Father Pierre-Jean De Smet (1801–1873)

Pierre-Jean De Smet was born in Belgium in 1801. He was inspired to join the Jesuits order of the Catholic Church after hearing a sermon appealing for men to become missionaries to the Indians of North America. De Smet accepted the calling. He sailed to the United States and entered the Jesuit **novitiate** in Maryland in 1821. He took his vows of priesthood at Florissant, Missouri, in 1827. Father De Smet (usually called Father Jean) was responsible for the establishment of many Catholic missions in the American West and undertook several hazardous journeys, often barely escaping with his life. He was involved in a shipwreck and was even attacked by a bear. Still, Father De Smet was a tireless and fearless missionary who converted many Native Americans to Catholicism. He was often called upon to assist the Office of Indian Affairs and the U.S. Army in their peace negotiations with different Native American tribes. Father De Smet died in St. Louis, Missouri, on May 23, 1873.

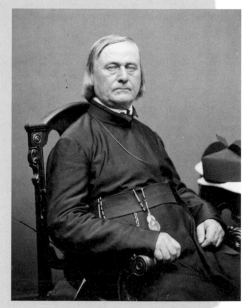

Father Pierre-Jean De Smet, shown in this photograph from the 1860s, was a Catholic priest, originally from Belgium, who worked tirelessly on behalf of Native Americans.

# The Treaty of 1868

After Father Jean and his interpreter left the Sioux camp, Sitting Bull had a change of heart. Although he trusted Father Jean, he still didn't trust the officials of the U.S. government. Instead of going to Fort Rice himself, Sitting Bull decided to send Gall, one of his fellow warriors, who had once been Sitting Bull's rival for power in the tribe. Sitting Bull knew that Gall had almost been killed by white soldiers, and, because of that, he was sure that Gall would not give in to whatever demands the U.S. government presented to him.

At Fort Rice, the government officials refused to listen to Gall. Instead, they suggested that the Sioux would find their lives easier if they gave up hunting and started farming for a living. In other words, the only thing they were really interested in was moving all remaining Indians onto reservations so that the white settlers could have their land. Sitting Bull had been right in his assessment of the government's true motives. Gall angrily refused, telling the officials that the whites should stop farming, kill their livestock, and go back across the ocean to the lands where they or their ancestors were born.

*Although he trusted Father Jean, he still didn't trust the officials of the U.S. government.*

Still, on July 2, 1868, Gall signed a treaty agreeing the attacks and fighting would stop. In exchange, the U.S. government promised that no white people could settle on land bounded by the North Platte River and the Bighorn Mountains. This vast territory included parts of the states of North Dakota, South Dakota, Nebraska, Wyoming, and Montana. What was more important for the Sioux, though, was that the treaty meant the sacred Black Hills could not be touched. Even so, Sitting Bull was

In 1868, Sitting Bull sent Gall (pictured here in 1885) to Fort Rice, thinking that Gall would never give in to the demands of the U.S. government representatives. But Gall did sign the Treaty of 1868, greatly angering Sitting Bull.

angry that Gall signed it at all. However, in the months following, life for Sitting Bull and his followers seemed to improve. Now that the Sioux leaders didn't have to spend as much time fighting the white settlers, they could concentrate on their daily lives. There were marriages, and there were successful hunts. Life seemed good again.

# CHAPTER 8

# The Black Hills Are Sacred

*I will sit here on the prairie and listen. Everybody knows my terms.*

By the year 1870, the U.S. government had convinced most of the Indian tribes of the Great Plains to move onto reservations. It used incentives—such as a promise of an easier life—as well as threats of what would happen if the tribes didn't comply. Even under such pressure, Sitting Bull still refused, steadfastly claiming that his people would forever remain free and live the life that *Wakan Tanka* had given them.

Not all of the leaders of the tribes of the Great Sioux Nation felt the same way, though. The powerful Oglala leader Red Cloud had met with U.S. officials and was now encouraging other Sioux to move to the reservation. This made Sitting Bull very angry. He thought Red Cloud's

In 1870, the powerful leader of the Oglala Sioux, Chief Red Cloud, angered Sitting Bull by encouraging the Sioux to move onto reservations. This photograph shows Red Cloud twenty-eight years later, at the age of seventy-seven.

influence could possibly convince the leaders of the other Sioux bands to follow his lead. Sitting Bull told the Hunkpapa that "the white people must have put bad medicine over Red Cloud's eyes to make him see everything and anything that pleased them."

## Breaking the Treaty

In 1872, just four years after the Treaty of 1868, Sitting Bull and his followers were once again involved in confrontations with the U.S. government. Officials had been sent to the area around the Yellowstone River to survey the land so that railroad tracks could be laid. The Sioux were angry that the railroad would run right through their land. No one had asked their permission for

This photograph shows American troops being sent to survey the land around the Yellowstone River so railroad tracks could be laid. Seeing this, the Sioux realized that the U.S. government was planning to break the Treaty of 1868.

this to be done. Sitting Bull couldn't believe that the government was going to do exactly what the Treaty of 1868 said it couldn't do. To him, it was inconceivable that U.S. government officials would be so arrogant as to break a solemn treaty because it was convenient for them to do so.

Some Sioux leaders, like Gall, took immediate action and began fighting the soldiers. Sitting Bull, though greatly saddened and very disappointed, tried to convince the other tribes that such confrontations would not gain them anything. But few outside the Hunkpapa band paid any attention to his words.

In August, relations between the Indians and the U.S. government began to deteriorate even more. One day, Gall and his warriors raced into camp, shouting that white soldiers were coming up the river, toward their camp. Sitting Bull decided it was time to meet them face-to-face and to tell them to leave Sioux land. The Hunkpapa had tried to honor the Treaty of 1868 and had refrained from recent battles with the U.S. Army. Surely his words would carry enough weight

*Sitting Bull decided it was time to meet them face-to-face and to tell them to leave Sioux land.*

with the government, and the soldiers would honor his request. Among the men Sitting Bull chose to accompany him was Crazy Horse, now a great warrior in his own right.

Sitting Bull and his party reached the cavalry camp early one morning. But before he could tell the soldiers why he was there, the nervous bluecoats opened fire, killing several of the Sioux warriors. Sitting Bull, Crazy Horse, and the remaining warriors took cover. For several hours, the Sioux fought bravely against the army's superior gun power. When the shooting stopped, Sitting Bull and his remaining men gathered up their dead and returned

Against the wishes of the Plains Indians, including the Sioux, railroad tracks were laid across the Great Plains, as shown in this lithograph from 1875.

to their camp. In the past, the warriors would have struck back with an attack, but Sitting Bull had not come for that purpose, and it was a matter of honor to respect that fact. On the way back, Sitting Bull and Crazy Horse made a pact. Never again would they do something that might provoke the bluecoats. If the soldiers attacked them, though, they would fight to the death.

Over the next two years, Sitting Bull and his people saw the railroad getting closer and closer to their land, but soon, a new problem arose.

## Gold in the Black Hills

On July 2, 1874, an exploratory expedition of **geologists** and U.S. Army troops left Fort Abraham Lincoln and headed for the Black Hills to look for gold and for land that was suitable for white settlements. The leader was Lieutenant Colonel George Armstrong Custer. After traveling for several weeks, Custer sent back reports saying that not only was the area perfect for farming but that some of the geologists were almost certain there was gold there. With that news, thousands of miners headed for the Black Hills, once again forgetting all about the Treaty of 1868.

When President Ulysses S. Grant sent a second expedition to the Black Hills in 1875, there were already hundreds of white miners digging for gold. Grant knew that it would be impossible to get these miners to leave the area—thereby honoring the Treaty of 1868—so instead, he sent his representatives to draw up a new agreement with the Sioux. The president was prepared to offer them four hundred thousand dollars a year for the right to mine in the Black Hills, or six million dollars to buy the land outright.

When gold was discovered in the Black Hills of South Dakota in 1874, white miners immediately rushed to the area, even though the U.S. government had promised the Sioux that this would not happen. This 1889 photograph shows three men panning for gold in a stream.

This was money that could keep many Sioux from living in poverty. However, the government had no idea where Sitting Bull's camp was located, so President Grant hired Frank Grouard, a white man, to help find it. Grouard had once lived among Sitting Bull's people, could speak the Sioux language, and most importantly knew where the chief could be found.

Grouard was tasked with getting Sitting Bull to go to the Red Cloud Agency, a reservation where many Sioux were already living, to discuss the government's offer. But Sitting Bull refused Grouard's request to discuss giving up the land. He told Grouard, whom he no longer trusted, that the Sioux would go to war if the whites tried to take the Black Hills from them. Grouard later said, "I never saw an Indian quite as mad as he was."

Although Sitting Bull refused to go, there were many other Sioux leaders who did show up at the Red Cloud Agency; the

To keep from starving, many Sioux moved onto government reservations, such as the Red Cloud Agency in Nebraska, shown in this lithograph from the 1870s. At the agency, they were given food, clothing, and shelter.

To the Sioux, there seemed to be no end to the number of white settlers crossing through or settling on their land, as shown in this colored lithograph from the 1870s.

government decided to go ahead with the meeting. But the representatives present were not prepared for the reception they received: Thousands of angry Indians surrounded them and told them in no uncertain terms that they wanted the white miners and the soldiers to leave the Black Hills at once. The agents returned to Washington, D.C., and informed President Grant that they had been unsuccessful in their negotiations with the Sioux.

The Black Hills wasn't the only area that was seeing an influx of white American settlers. Thousands more were heading even farther west across the Great Plains. Since they, too, needed food, they often killed the buffalo, but usually shot more animals than they needed and took only part of the meat, leaving the rest to be picked over by **scavengers**. The white settlers were slowly **decimating** the herds. The main source of food for the Indians of the plains was disappearing, and more and more of the Native people began to starve. To avoid starvation, many of the tribes moved onto the reservations, where they were given food, clothing, and shelter, but Sitting Bull still refused. He didn't want to live among the "agency Indians," as he called them, so he and his Hunkpapa followers decided to remain in the Black Hills.

## "Hostile" Indians

Sitting Bull's attitude angered officials in Washington. They decided to order all Indians to move to government reservations by January 31, 1876. Those Indians who didn't comply with the government's request would be considered "hostile," and they would be taken prisoner by U.S. Army troops and moved onto the reservations by force.

Unfortunately, this government order didn't reach many of the agencies or camps until the latter part of December 1875. By then, winter storms were raging and deep snow covered most of the Great Plains. For those tribes who did receive the order, it was impossible to dismantle the tepees, pack up everything on horses, and ride through blizzards to the nearest reservation.

It was already January when Sitting Bull received the news. He told the messenger who delivered it that he would think about the request but that he and his followers could do nothing until the spring. This was not what the government wanted to hear. In February of 1876, Sitting Bull and the remaining Sioux were declared "hostile Indians."

In March, the government ordered General George Crook and his soldiers to leave Fort Fetterman in Wyoming and capture Crazy Horse and his

*In February of 1876, Sitting Bull and the remaining Sioux were declared "hostile Indians."*

Oglala warriors—the band thought to be causing the government the most trouble with their hit-and-run missions against U.S.

Army troops. Frank Grouard was acting as a scout for the troops. With the winter storms still raging, though, and with their supplies running low, General Crook decided they would soon have to return to Fort Fetterman if they didn't find the Indians.

On March 17, Grouard led the troops to an Indian settlement on the banks of the Powder River. Grouard told General Crook that this was Crazy Horse's camp. He was wrong. It was another camp of Oglala and Cheyenne. The soldiers attacked the camp, burning the tepees and driving away the prized horses, but the warriors fought back and forced the soldiers to retreat. General Crook decided that it was time to return to Fort Fetterman.

## Fighting the White Man—Again

The surviving Oglala and Cheyenne managed to find some of their horses, but they were without shelter and food, so they made their way through a blizzard to where Crazy Horse was actually camped.

Crazy Horse and his followers headed north to find Sitting Bull. His camp was now on the Tongue River, in what is today the state of Wyoming. When Sitting Bull heard about the attack on the Oglala and Cheyenne camp, he told Crazy Horse that if they didn't stand together, they would be destroyed.

Runners from the various camps began spreading the word that all Indians west of the Missouri River should come to the big bend of the Rosebud River, in what is today the state of Montana. Before long, the tribes began to make their ways there. Even Indians from the reservations came, bringing with them guns and bullets. By June, over fifteen thousand Native people had gathered.

# Crazy Horse (c. 1842–1877)

Crazy Horse was a highly respected war leader of the Oglala Sioux. He fought against the U.S. government in an effort to preserve the traditions and values of the Sioux way of life. He was born around 1842 and was given the name "Light Hair" because his hair and skin were lighter than the rest of the tribe. His father, who was also named Crazy Horse, gave his name to his son when he turned eighteen. Crazy Horse did not always follow the usual Sioux customs of wearing face paint and war bonnets during battles, nor did he cover himself with dust, the way many warriors did, but he gained a reputation as a fierce warrior. In 1866, Crazy Horse led one thousand warriors against the U.S. Cavalry at Fort Phil Kearny. In 1877, while attempting to escape arrest by soldiers of the U.S. Army, Crazy Horse was bayoneted and later died from his wounds.

Crazy Horse, shown here in full battle dress, was a respected war leader of the Oglala Sioux and fought many battles alongside Sitting Bull.

# CHAPTER 9

# Seeing into the Future

*These dead soldiers who are coming are the gifts of* Wakan Tanka.

The leaders of the different bands now wanted to determine individually how they would deal with the U.S. government. Sitting Bull was no longer the supreme war chief of the united Great Sioux Nation, but he was still considered a very important chief, and his word carried a lot of weight.

At night, Sitting Bull and the other chiefs, including Gall, Crazy Horse, Two Moons, and Spotted Eagle, sat in a circle around what was called a council fire and talked. The fact that they also smoked the war pipe together meant that they were united against the white settlers who were trying to steal their land.

Still limping from the Crow-inflicted wound to his foot, Sitting Bull would walk

Spotted Eagle, shown here in a photograph from the early 1900s, often smoked a war pipe with Sitting Bull and other Sioux chiefs to show that he was united with them in fighting the white settlers.

around the huge camp during the day, telling everyone how important it was to continue to fight so they could keep what had been given to them by *Wakan Tanka*. He admonished the warriors he encountered always to be brave. The people still listened to his words.

## The Sun Dance and Vision

At the beginning of June, the tribes began to get ready for that year's Sun Dance. Although Sitting Bull's body was covered with many scars from previous Sun Dances, he believed that his participation in the one upcoming would be the most important of his lifetime. Earlier in the year, Sitting Bull had promised *Wakan Tanka* that a red blanket of blood would flow from his body if the Great Spirit would help the Native people chase the white man away from their lands. Now, in fulfillment of this promise, Sitting Bull would give one hundred pieces of his skin, to be cut from his own arms, as part of the Sun Dance ceremony. To Sioux warriors, enduring such pain showed *Wakan Tanka* they were willing to sacrifice their bodies in exchange for his blessings and guidance.

Sitting Bull chose his adopted brother, Stays-Back—now called Jumping Bull, in honor of Sitting Bull's father—to perform the cutting ceremony. Using a very sharp knife and an awl, Jumping Bull cut away the pieces from Sitting Bull's arms. Although Sitting Bull was soon covered with his own blood, he never once flinched or cried out in pain.

With the center pole in place, covered with decorations, and the body preparations finished, the dancing began. Sitting Bull was joined by several other warriors. Together, they danced and chanted under the hot sun. Never stopping once, not even to eat, they continued under the bright stars.

After a day and a half, Sitting Bull went into a **trance** and fell to the ground.

It was at this moment that Sitting Bull had his most famous vision. He saw hundreds of bluecoats falling to earth around him. Sitting Bull also heard a voice telling him that the bluecoats had no ears. Right away, he knew the meaning of this vision. He no longer needed a shaman to interpret it for him. That the soldiers had no ears meant they refused to listen to him and the other chiefs, and that they were falling meant they were dying. Because the bluecoats were falling into the camp where the different tribes had gathered, Sitting Bull interpreted that to mean they would be killed by Indians.

*Now, in fulfillment of this promise, Sitting Bull would give one hundred pieces of his skin.*

When Sitting Bull woke from his trance, he told the others about his vision. They all felt that Sitting Bull could foretell the future. His vision filled them with hope that they would be victorious over the bluecoats—and that the white settlers would have to leave their land if they wanted to live. All of the chiefs were encouraged by this vision and began preparing their tribes for battle.

## Battle of Rosebud River

Unbeknownst to Sitting Bull and the thousands of Indians gathered on the banks of the Rosebud River, the U.S. Army had been making battle plans, too. In May of that year, a month before the Sun Dance, the generals had put together a three-part attack against the tribes, with General Crook, Colonel John Gibbon, and General Alfred Terry each commanding a **column of troops.**

Colonel John Gibbon, pictured here in a photograph from the late 1800s, was one of the U.S. Army commanders in charge of what was to be a three-pronged attack against the thousands of Sioux camped along the Rosebud River.

Lieutenant Colonel George Armstrong Custer would be leading a group of General Terry's troops. To the tribes of the plains, he was known as "Long Hair" because of his long blond locks. The plan called for each group of soldiers to attack the tribes from a different point. By the time the Sun Dance was over, the U.S. Army was ready.

A few days after Sitting Bull had his vision, on June 17, a hunting party of Cheyenne left the camp on the Rosebud to look for buffalo. The men had only been gone a short time when they all came racing back with the news that there were bluecoats camped a few miles downstream.

This was all Sitting Bull needed to know. He and Crazy Horse, leading all the Sioux bands, headed off to do battle with the bluecoats. Before long, though, Sitting Bull withdrew to the rear of the column. He wasn't as young as he used to be, and his age was beginning to show. The Sun Dance had also exhausted him. Crazy Horse became the leader of the warriors as they continued on toward the army encampment. Before they got there, however, they encountered some of their longtime enemies, the Crow and the Shoshone, who were now **allied** with the U.S. Army. Crazy Horse and his men quickly killed some of them and

When the Battle of Rosebud River started, the Sioux used unconventional battle tactics, as shown in this 1876 newspaper lithograph. They rode quickly into the soldiers' camp, taunted them mercilessly, and then rapidly fled to the safety of the surrounding brush.

forced the others to retreat. Excited by this triumph, they now raced for the bluecoats.

When the Sioux reached the army's encampment on the banks of the Rosebud River, the troops, under the command of General Crook, immediately starting firing at them, but Crazy Horse was determined to win this battle. He came up with a new plan of attack. The Sioux warriors began racing into and around the encampment of bluecoats, leaning low on the sides of their horses to avoid being in the sights of the soldiers' rifles. Yelling and riding swiftly, the Native warriors taunted the soldiers and then

General George Crook, shown in this photograph from the late 1800s, was in command of the unit that the Sioux attacked first on the Rosebud River.

retreated so fast that the soldiers didn't know what was happening. This tactic disoriented the American troops.

General Crook had never seen anything like it before. He didn't know how to fight an enemy who wasn't challenging them in the expected way. At the end of the day, Crook knew that there was no way he could win this battle. He led his men in retreat back to their base camp on Goose Creek, several miles away, where they would wait until either Colonel Gibbon, General Terry, or Lieutenant Colonel Custer returned. He planned to tell them that his small force of soldiers was no match for the Indians he had just tried to fight.

## Moving to a New Site

When Crazy Horse and his warriors returned to their camp on the Rosebud River, some of the Indians wondered if Sitting Bull's vision had been fulfilled since the bluecoats had been defeated. But Sitting Bull didn't believe it had been. The Sioux were somewhat disappointed, but they trusted what Sitting Bull had told them and vowed to make sure they were ready when it was time for the vision to be fulfilled.

With so many people in the camp, all the wild animals in the area were killed for food, and the horses ate all the surrounding grass. As he often did, Sitting Bull prayed, "*Wakan Tanka*, save me and give me all my wild game animals. Bring them near to me, so that my people may have plenty to eat this winter." Some time later, several Sioux scouts returned to camp with the news that there was a valley to the west with plenty of game to hunt and plenty of sweet grass for the horses to graze on.

Sitting Bull knew of this place. It was called the valley of the Little Bighorn. The tribes all packed up their belongings and headed in that direction.

# CHAPTER 10

# Battle of the Little Bighorn

*Warriors, we have everything to fight for, and if we are defeated we shall have nothing to live for; therefore let us fight like brave men.*

When all of the tribes finally arrived in the valley of the Little Bighorn, the new camp spread out for more than three miles along the banks of the Little Bighorn River. There were almost ten thousand people, about a third of whom were warriors who wanted nothing more than to fight the white soldiers. Until that time came, though, life continued as it always had, no matter where the Sioux were camped. The men went hunting, the women searched for wild vegetables and fruit, and the children played in the river. At night, after the evening meal, everyone gathered around campfires to tell stories.

On some evenings, when the chiefs deemed it necessary, they would go to one of their tepees and hold a council meeting. Sitting Bull was always the first to be

Sitting Bull holds council with the other chiefs in this lithograph from the late 1800s.

asked what was on his mind. From that, other discussions followed, as the chiefs talked about how to keep the U.S. government from forcing the Native people to change their old ways.

While the Plains Indians were making their plans, the U.S. Army was also making their plans to conquer all the tribes.

## An Unwise Decision

On June 22, 1876, Lieutenant Colonel George Custer and the almost seven hundred troops he commanded in the Seventh Cavalry Regiment marched along the banks of the Rosebud River in hopes of finding Sitting Bull's camp. Custer was primed for battle and had no doubt that his men, with their superior training and weapons, could defeat these Sioux warriors.

Some Crow scouts that Custer had sent on ahead came back with the news that the Indians had moved but that the trail they had taken could be easily followed. But the scouts also believed that the Sioux force was too large, probably numbering in the thousands, for Custer and his men to battle alone. They suggested that Custer slow his march and proceed very carefully. But Custer felt if he followed the advice of his scouts, the Indians would escape— and most importantly, the glory and honor he and his men wanted from such an

Lieutenant Colonel George Armstrong Custer is shown in this photograph taken sometime during the American Civil War (1861–1865). He was in charge of the ill-fated attack on the Sioux at the Battle of the Little Bighorn.

engagement would be denied them. Custer told his scouts that he had no intention of waiting. He continued to follow the trail, which headed toward the valley of the Little Bighorn.

Custer was so obsessed with finding his foes that he forced his men to ride night and day, seldom allowing them to stop to rest or to eat. Finally, on the morning of June 25, they reached a ridge overlooking the valley of the Little Bighorn. White Man Runs Him, a scout, told Custer that he should wait for reinforcements because the size of the Sioux encampment was too large. Custer paid no attention to the advice.

By noon, Custer had organized his troops into three different attack groups. The first group was to be commanded by Captain Frederick W. Benteen, the second by Major Marcus Reno, and the third by Custer himself. Custer ordered Captain Benteen to take his troops into the hills southeast of the Indian camp. Custer and Reno would then proceed down into the valley, where they would split up, with Reno's men crossing the river and attacking the camp from the south and Custer's crossing the river and attacking the camp from the east.

*Custer was primed for battle and had no doubt that his men . . . could defeat these Sioux warriors.*

Unbeknownst to Custer, some of the women from the camp had been digging for turnips near the river and had spotted a number of the troops. Right away, they ran to warn Sitting Bull and the other chiefs. By the time Major Reno began his attack from the south, the Sioux were ready to fight. Sitting Bull, gun in hand, jumped onto his horse and led his Hunkpapa warriors to confront Reno and his men. But Sitting Bull once again realized that he no longer had the physical strength to go into battle. So he said to One Bull, one of his own warriors, "You will take my place

# White Man Runs Him (c. 1858–1929)

White Man Runs Him was a Crow Indian scout who served with George Armstrong Custer. Although his account of the Battle of the Little Bighorn was largely forgotten for almost a hundred years, it has now proved invaluable to modern historians.

On June 25, 1876, he accompanied Custer to the Crow's Nest, a rock formation which overlooked the Little Bighorn valley, so they could assess the situation. White Man Runs Him and the other scouts advised Custer to wait for reinforcements, but Custer ignored them and prepared to attack the Sioux camp. The Crow scouts then went to another ridge overlooking what would be the battlefield, where they witnessed the event. It was only toward the end of the twentieth century that historians began to recognize Native American accounts of the battles they fought with the U.S. Army during the late 1800s. White Man Runs Him lived the remainder of his life on the Crow reservation just a few miles from the site of the famous battle. He died there in 1929.

Shown in this photograph from the early 1900s, White Man Runs Him was one of General Custer's Crow scouts who told him to wait for reinforcements before attacking the Sioux camped along the Little Bighorn River. Custer ignored his advice.

and go out and meet the soldiers that are attacking us. Parley with them if you can. If they are willing, tell them I will talk peace with them." Unfortunately for both sides, events had gone too far to be stopped.

Major Reno was taken by surprise at the size and the strength of the Sioux fighting force. He ordered his men to dismount and fight the Indians from the ground, thinking his troops would be a harder target to hit than if they were on their horses, but the **strategy** didn't work, and many white soldiers were killed. Knowing they wouldn't last much longer, Reno ordered the remaining troops back onto their horses and had them recross the Little Bighorn River, where they sought shelter in the trees.

The Sioux only had a short time to enjoy their quick victory over the bluecoats when they saw a cloud of dust coming from the east. The sound of a bugle told them that other soldiers were now attacking the camp from that direction. Rather than the quick victory they thought they had, the battle was just beginning!

Major Marcus Reno, shown in this photograph from the late 1800s, immediately ordered his men back across the river upon seeing the size of the Sioux fighting force camped along the Little Bighorn River.

# Custer's Last Stand

As his men raced through the Indian camp from the east, Custer was now stunned at how large it was. He knew right away that he had made a serious mistake by attacking it without waiting for reinforcements. He sent a runner to tell Captain Benteen to attack immediately.

Custer's command would go unanswered, though, because on his way down into the valley, Captain Benteen had seen Major Reno's retreat and had rushed to his aid right away. Instead of joining Custer, he made the decision to help Major Reno and his men move back across the Little Bighorn River.

Sitting Bull was now joined by Gall and Crazy Horse, who had arrived with their men from opposite sides of the encampment. He was glad to have the younger warriors with him. Although Sitting Bull still wanted to be in the midst of battle, he was smart enough to know that his age could be a hindrance. Again he gradually withdrew to the rear, urging the warriors to destroy the bluecoats once and for all.

Once Custer and his men had neared the east side of the Little Bighorn River, the warriors who lived in tepees on the northern edge of the village, mostly Cheyenne, leaped onto their

When Captain Frederick W. Benteen saw Major Marcus Reno retreating across the Little Bighorn River, he ordered his men to follow instead of joining Custer. Benteen is shown here in a photograph from the late 1800s.

horses and began firing their guns at the soldiers. Across the river from Custer and his troops lay the rest of the huge camp, and Custer could see thousands of other warriors, whooping war cries with tomahawks raised. There was no escape in any direction.

Custer was sure his men were as horrified at what they were witnessing as he was, but there was nothing else to do except fight as long and as hard as they could against such overwhelming odds. Custer shouted for his men to dismount and fire from the ground.

Although Custer's men put up a hard fight, they never had a chance, and in the end, Custer's arrogance for wanting a glorious victory for himself and his troops proved to be his undoing. When the fighting was finally over, neither Custer nor any of his men were alive.

In a highly romanticized lithograph from 1889, Lieutenant Colonel George Armstrong Custer is making a brave stand, firing guns in both hands, against the attacking Sioux at the Battle of the Little Bighorn.

Battle of the
Little Bighorn
June 25, 1876

Crazy Horse

Custer

Gall

Benteen

Reno

Route of Custer
Route of Reno
Route of Benteen
Routes of the Sioux
△ Indian village
Battle

MONTANA
WYOMING

0        10 MI
0        20 KM

This map shows the Battle of the Little Bighorn and how Custer's entire 7th Cavalry Regiment was wiped out. It shows Benteen's route as he went to aid the retreating Reno, leaving Custer alone to fight against thousands of Sioux warriors led by Crazy Horse from the north and Gall from the southwest.

When Sitting Bull saw some of the Sioux warriors stealing the personal belongings from the dead soldiers, he ordered them to stop. He told them that if they used anything that belonged to a white man, they would become like him. That night, the people in the camp mourned the warriors who had died fighting by singing songs to *Wakan Tanka* about their heroic deeds in battle. Afterward, everyone began praising Sitting Bull for his vision and for his battle leadership, but he would not listen to them, for he knew that this one victory would not stop the violence.

Now, Sitting Bull told the people, the white men would be angrier than ever.

# Little Bighorn Battlefield National Monument

The Little Bighorn Battlefield National Monument commemorates one of the most significant battles in American history, which took place on June 25 and June 26 in 1876. It is located near Crow Agency, a reservation in the state of Montana. In 1879, the Little Bighorn Battlefield became a national cemetery. In 1881, a memorial to the Seventh Cavalry soldiers and the U.S. Indian scouts who were killed in the battle was erected over the mass grave. To also honor the Native American warriors who died in the battle, the U.S. Congress ordered the construction of an additional memorial in 1991.

The Indian Memorial at the Little Bighorn Battlefield National Monument features a bronze aboriginal sculpture of the Spirit Warriors.

# CHAPTER 11

# Making a Home in Canada

*We have two ways to go: to the land of the Grandmother, or to the land of the Spaniards.*

A t the same time that the Sioux were mourning their dead warriors and wondering what would happen to them next, Major Reno and Captain Benteen were urging their troops to work faster as they dug trenches in the hard dirt of the hills, so they could be in position to fight by dawn. Feeling totally helpless to do anything, the two commanders were sure that the Sioux would attack them next. There was no thought of riding back to one of the nearest forts on their own. They were exhausted. At the very least, they believed they were in an area where the terrain would offer them a little safety until other troops hopefully arrived—either to help them fight the Sioux or to escort them back to Fort Abraham Lincoln.

When the sun rose the next morning on June 26, fighting began again and continued for several hours. Reno and Benteen's men were exhausted from fighting and lack of water. The fighting continued until noontime, when the Indians suddenly stopped attacking. Reno and Benteen were confused by this sudden withdrawal and thought it was some kind of a trick. When Sioux scouts raced into the camp with the news that a large column of soldiers was headed toward them, Sitting Bull and the other chiefs decided they would not stay and fight. Instead, they would gather up their possessions and head up farther into the Big Horn Mountains.

## Into the Mountains

This new column of soldiers was under the command of Colonel Gibbon and General Terry. When their advanced scouts raced back to them to relay the news that Custer and all his men had been massacred, the generals found it hard to believe. The next day, June 27, when the column reached Reno and Benteen, the site of the battle was even worse than Gibbon and Terry had imagined. They immediately ordered their men to bury the dead soldiers. After that, they returned to Fort Abraham Lincoln.

After moving their camp to the Big Horn Mountains, Sitting Bull and the chiefs held a council to decide what to do next. Their

Last Stand Hill at the Little Bighorn National Monument is dotted with the gravestones of Custer and members of the 7th Cavalry who fell at this site in 1876.

mood was somber, not triumphant, and they had no interest in killing more white men. They were all very much aware that the white soldiers would keep coming and coming until the last Sioux was dead.

When the news of Custer's defeat reached the rest of the country, newspapers declared in bold headlines that it had been a horrible massacre by what reporters described as bloodthirsty savages.

*Their mood was somber, not triumphant, and they had no interest in killing more white men.*

White Americans were outraged and demanded that the government exact a heavy price on the Indians for what they had done. In ordinary terms, that meant moving them all onto reservations and killing the ones who refused.

The U.S. government acted swiftly, but it wasn't fast enough to capture either Sitting Bull or the other chiefs who had been at the Battle of the Little Bighorn. Still, the government took action against as many Indians as it could find. It captured and imprisoned men, women, and children. By July, even the Sioux who were already living on reservations were declared **prisoners of war**.

Shortly afterward, the government announced that since the Indians had violated the Treaty of 1868 by going to war with the United States, a huge tract of what was formerly Indian land, including the Black Hills and the Powder River, was now under American control. It didn't matter that the battle at Little Bighorn had been started by the U.S. Army and that the government had long ago violated the same treaty by allowing white settlers and miners to settle in the "protected" Indian areas. Although most of the Indians living on reservations accepted what they thought to be inevitable results, Sitting Bull refused. He told anyone who would listen, "I did not hunt Custer. I thought I had a right to protect my own women and children. If he had taken our village he would have killed our women and children. It was a fair fight."

During the rest of the summer and into the fall, Sitting Bull and the warriors he still had under his command fought several minor battles with the U.S. Army. Finally, Sitting Bull came to the conclusion that, no matter how long and hard he fought the bluecoats, he and his people would never again be allowed to live in peace in the Black Hills. He started thinking about where he could now move his people.

## Sitting Bull's Refusal

During a council meeting one evening, Sitting Bull told his warriors that there were only two directions they could take: south to Mexico, to live in the land of the Spanish speakers, or north to Canada, the home of the Grandmother. This was the

Queen Victoria, photographed in 1862, ruled the British Empire, which included Canada, for eighty-two years. The Sioux called her "Grandmother."

name Native Americans called Queen Victoria, who ruled Canada from her throne in Great Britain.

In October of 1876, before Sitting Bull had made a decision on the direction they would travel, there was another attempt by the U.S. government to make peace with the Indians who had refused to move to the reservations. General Nelson A. Miles met with Sitting Bull and some of his warriors out on the prairie, several miles from Sitting Bull's camp, to try to reason with him. Although both men were polite to each other, it was obvious from the start that nothing would be accomplished. Almost immediately, Sitting Bull demanded to know why the bluecoats were still on Indian land. Ignoring Sitting Bull's question, Miles told him that he had orders to take Sitting Bull and his followers to a reservation. He ordered Sitting Bull to command his warriors to give up their weapons without a fight and for the entire tribe to follow the soldiers who were waiting just a few hundred yards away.

Sitting Bull, of course, refused. He told Miles that *Wakan Tanka* had made him a free Indian, not a reservation Indian, and that he would always be a free Indian. Miles, in turn, told Sitting Bull that if he and his followers did not accept the government's terms, the army would open fire.

Even after Sitting Bull's death, General Nelson A. Miles tried to gain military control over the Sioux. This 1891 photograph shows ten Lakota chiefs at a council they had with Miles.

Sitting Bull was prepared for such a threat. Immediately, he and the other warriors raced for their horses and headed off onto the prairie where they set fires, hoping to stop the soldiers, but their plan didn't work. The soldiers followed them, and the battle continued.

By the next day, both sides were exhausted, and while Sitting Bull still refused to report to the reservation, over two thousand of the people from his camp decided they would, because they were simply tired of fighting. When they approached the cavalry troops with a white flag of truce, Sitting Bull knew that it was useless to try to stop them. Although Sitting Bull was still free, most of his warriors were gone.

With his remaining few hundred followers, Sitting Bull barely survived the harsh winter. Most of the buffalo were gone by now, so they had little fresh meat, and when the spring rains came, the river flooded and washed away their tepees. Sitting Bull could see that his people had almost reached the point where they didn't care what happened to them.

## The New Home

Sitting Bull and his small band finally headed north to Canada. Although it grieved him to leave his sacred land, the great chief and his group of tired Native people straggled across the border into Canada in May of 1877. They traveled about sixty miles up the White Mud Valley and set up their first camp near Pinto Horse Butte in the present-day province of Saskatchewan. They were soon visited by the North West Mounted Police—the arm of the law charged with keeping order in the Canadian West. The troops were under the command of Major James M. Walsh, who laid down the law to Sitting Bull. The new arrivals were expected to obey the laws of Canada. That meant they weren't allowed to steal horses from neighboring Indian tribes. Walsh also told Sitting Bull that they were forbidden to cross back into the United States to make raids there, because the Canadian government didn't want to sour its relations with its powerful neighbor to the south.

Shown here is an 1873 portrait of Major James Morrow Walsh of the North West Mounted Police. He was one of the few government officials Sitting Bull ever trusted.

# North West Mounted Police

In 1873, the North West Mounted Police—forerunner of today's Royal Canadian Mounted Police—was created by an act of the Canadian Parliament. The constables who were charged with maintaining peace and order in the Canadian West wore as their daily uniform a brilliant red serge tunic. Sir John A. Macdonald, Canada's first prime minister, modeled the force's structure after the Royal Irish Constabulary, but the equipment and military tactics would be those used by the U.S. Cavalry. According to some sources, the red uniforms were meant to distinguish the Canadian forces from the blue-coated U.S. cavalrymen. For the most part, Sitting Bull and his followers had peaceful relations with the North West Mounted Police.

An 1873 pen and ink drawing shows the North West Mounted Police, who were the equivalent of the U.S. Cavalry.

Sitting Bull agreed to the terms presented by Walsh. He was tired, and he didn't think he could fight anymore. Although he missed his sacred land, he had already accepted the idea that he would live out the rest of his life in Canada and be buried in this alien country. What Sitting Bull didn't know was that the governments of Canada and the United States had other plans. The Canadian government was getting nervous that its Indian population had increased dramatically, and the U.S. government wanted Sitting Bull back so they could keep him and his followers under control.

In 1877, General Terry (from the Battle of the Little Bighorn) was sent to Canada to negotiate with Sitting Bull. Terry told him

In this 1877 magazine engraving, Sitting Bull is shown giving advice to Canadian officials on how his people should be treated.

that if he and his people would agree to return to the United States and to live on a reservation, no one would be punished. Sitting Bull told Terry that for sixty-four years the U.S. government had treated his people badly, finally forcing them to cross the border into Canada to live in peace. As far as he was concerned, this was now their home.

## Surrendering for His People

Over the next few years, life in Canada became more and more difficult for Sitting Bull and his followers. For one thing, the Canadian government would not give them any food—unlike the U.S. government that had promised to provide Native Americans with provisions. The buffalo were scarce on the Canadian side of the border, and if Sitting Bull or his warriors crossed over into the United States to hunt, the bluecoats shot at them. More and more of Sitting Bull's followers began to cross back over the border, telling the soldiers that they were ready to live on the reservations. Sitting Bull was soon left with only old people and parentless children—a difficult situation, because there was no one left to hunt and forage for food.

By the summer of 1881, Sitting Bull knew he would finally have to make a decision about how he and his remaining followers would survive. When he approached officials of the Canadian government about giving them a reservation in Canada, not only did they refuse, but they told him that he and his people were no longer welcome in Canada and had to return to the United States. Sitting Bull realized that he had at last been defeated.

*Over the next few years, life in Canada became more and more difficult for Sitting Bull and his followers.*

On July 19, Sitting Bull and 107 of his followers reached Fort Buford in the present-day state of North Dakota. Soldiers and officials from the U.S. government were there to meet them, having been alerted by the Canadian authorities. The next day, when Sitting Bull officially surrendered, he gave his rifle to his young son, Crow Foot, who had been born on the eve of the Battle of the Little Bighorn. Tired and dispirited and knowing that he needed to think of his family's future, Sitting Bull said, "I surrender this rifle to you through my young son, whom I desire to teach in this manner now that he has become a friend of the Americans. I wish him to learn the habits of the whites and to be educated as their sons are educated. I wish it to be remembered that I was the last man of my tribe to surrender my rifle."

On July 20, 1881, Sitting Bull surrendered at Fort Buford. He did so by handing his rifle to his son, Crow Foot, shown in this late 1800s photograph, who then gave the weapon to the American authorities.

# CHAPTER 12

# A New Way of Life

*I am ready to make a peace.*

After Sitting Bull surrendered, the government authorities at Fort Buford promised that he would be allowed to stay in his sacred Sioux homeland. They also told him that before long he would be reunited with his followers who had previously surrendered and were now living on reservations. The authorities hoped that by extending these generous promises, Sitting Bull wouldn't cause them any trouble. Sitting Bull wanted to believe his captors. The terms were exactly what he had asked of *Wakan Tanka*. But, as with all the other promises he had been given, this one was broken, too. In fact, within weeks of his surrender, Sitting Bull and some of his followers were taken as prisoners of war to Fort Randall in South Dakota.

Sitting Bull had fully expected to be killed once he had reentered the United States from Canada. But having reached Fort Randall alive and well, he was even more astonished when the army officers posted there

After Sitting Bull surrendered to American authorities in 1881, he and his followers were taken as prisoners of war to Fort Randall. This 1882 photograph shows bundles of food supplies which had just arrived there for distribution to the Sioux.

treated him with respect and allowed him to take charge of the small group of followers who had accompanied him to the fort.

## Overcoming Humiliation

In 1883, when Sitting Bull and his small band were sent to the Standing Rock Reservation in the southern part of North Dakota, their lives immediately changed for the worse. The officer in charge of the reservation, Major James McLaughlin, let it be known that he wasn't impressed with Sitting Bull. Right away, McLaughlin put Sitting Bull to work doing farm labor, a humiliating experience for a man who had once been a great hunter and was held in such high esteem by his people. Sitting Bull had encountered men like McLaughlin before, and he knew that what the major really wanted was to show Sitting Bull that McLaughlin was the more powerful of the two. He wanted to break Sitting Bull's spirit and force the famous chief to beg for whatever he needed. Sitting Bull would have no part of this. He continued to fight hard to preserve his leadership and to continue as many of the Sioux traditions as possible—especially the religious ceremonies and the vision quest for young boys.

As much as McLaughlin tried to diminish Sitting Bull's power, events conspired against the bitter officer. To McLaughlin's dismay, Sitting Bull, who was still famous, was invited to participate in the celebrations honoring the opening of the Northern Pacific Railroad. In a bit of irony, it was the building of the railroad that had begun the major conflicts between the Sioux and the U.S. government.

At the ceremony, Sitting Bull delivered a speech, as he had been requested to do, but he delivered it in his own language. He said, "I hate all the white people. You are thieves and liars. You have taken away our land and made us outcasts." The stunned

Sitting Bull spoke at the 1883 celebration of the completion of the Northern Pacific Railroad. One of its brochures from this period advertises the Yellowstone Park route to Puget Sound (in Washington state) and Alaska.

interpreter, knowing he couldn't allow the people to hear what Sitting Bull was actually saying, simply made up an entirely new speech—one that showed how the Indians and whites were now friends. At the end, the crowd gave Sitting Bull a standing ovation.

Much to his own surprise, Sitting Bull was soon struck with a desire to see more of the white man's world. It continually astonished him, and he felt both drawn to and repelled by it. He went on a tour of several American cities as the guest of men who had previously been his enemies. Sitting Bull was an object of curiosity and was often introduced as "the slayer of General Custer." Instead of drawing the anger of the crowd, everyone tried to get closer to him, as if they couldn't believe they were in the presence of such a powerful person.

## Joining the Wild West Show

A year later, in the summer of 1885, Buffalo Bill Cody, a showman, convinced Sitting Bull to join his traveling Wild West Show. Sitting Bull was promised fifty dollars a week for his performance—an enormous amount of money at the time.

Besides the money, Sitting Bull saw it as a chance to see the rest of the United States in relative safety. A typical show presented Sitting Bull as a famous Lakota chief. Dressed in his Indian finery, he usually sat on a horse and watched the performances.

He never participated in the staged attacks on white towns, as did the other Indians in the show, who played the part of bloodthirsty **renegades**. Buffalo Bill and the bluecoats would then ride in to save the white settlers from the Indian attacks. When Sitting Bull was asked to speak to the crowds, though, he did. In the Lakota language, he talked about peace and of his desire to get along

*. . . Buffalo Bill Cody, a showman, convinced Sitting Bull to join his traveling Wild West Show.*

with Americans, but the translators always made the people believe that he was telling them bloodcurdling accounts of how the Sioux had massacred the U.S. Cavalry at the Battle of the Little Bighorn.

For his part, Sitting Bull knew exactly what he was doing and felt amused at what was happening, not **demeaned**. Slowly but surely, he was beginning to understand how the minds of the white people worked. Things were either good or bad, black or white—there was no middle ground. For his people to survive, Sitting Bull had to know how the white man viewed the world around him.

When Sitting Bull rode into the arena, the crowds sometimes booed him, but he kept his dignity—about the only thing he had left—and played his role well. Sitting Bull even received top billing over the other famous member of the troupe, Annie Oakley, a well-known sharpshooter of the period. Sitting Bull had once seen her at a performance in St. Paul, Minnesota, before he joined the Wild West Show. He was so impressed with what Oakley could do, he called her "Little Sure Shot" and even

Annie Oakley and Sitting Bull became close friends when they both appeared in Buffalo Bill's Wild West Show. This 1899 photograph shows her with one of her rifles and some of her sharpshooting medals.

"adopted" her as his daughter. Oakley was also impressed with Sitting Bull, not just because he was a famous Sioux chief who had done great things for his people, but because he didn't keep the money he earned for himself. Instead, he gave it to the poor children who came around to see him after each performance.

When Sitting Bull finally decided that he no longer wanted to tour the United States with the Wild West Show, Buffalo Bill gave him two gifts to show his deep appreciation: his favorite gray circus horse that could perform many tricks and a white sombrero.

This 1885 publicity photograph promoted Sitting Bull's appearances in Buffalo Bill's Wild West Show.

In 1887, Buffalo Bill was invited to take his Wild West Show to Europe. He contacted Sitting Bull and pleaded with him to go. Cody knew that with the great chief as part of his show he would pack all the show arenas of Europe. Sitting Bull turned down the request, telling Cody he had decided it wasn't good for him or his people. He felt it would reawaken the hatred of whites for all things Indian. He added that he was also needed at Standing Rock because he had begun to hear more talk of taking away additional Indian land.

# Buffalo Bill's Wild West Show

William F. Cody was already a famous Indian scout and buffalo hunter when he met writer E. Z. C. Judson in the summer of 1869. Using Cody's adventures, Judson created the character of Buffalo Bill and made him the hero in several of his "dime novels"—cheaply printed books that were exciting to read but had no particular literary value. Soon, everyone in the United States had heard of William F. "Buffalo Bill" Cody. After Cody saw a play in New York based on his life, he decided to try his own hand at show business. After several moderately successful attempts, Cody came up with the idea of a Wild West Show. Its purpose was to entertain people and educate them about America's frontier. In 1886, Buffalo Bill's show performed at New York City's Madison Square Garden with Annie Oakley, the famous markswoman; trick riders; ropers; and more than one hundred Indians. Cody's Wild West Show was such a success in Great Britain that Queen Victoria saw it three times!

In the late 1800s, young people could read about Buffalo Bill's exciting adventures in what were called "dime novels," like the one shown here.

# CHAPTER 13

# The Ghost Dance

*The farther my people keep away from the whites the better I shall be satisfied.*

In 1888, the talk Sitting Bull had been hearing turned to action when representatives from the Office of Indian Affairs in Washington told the Indians that the government wanted to divide the Sioux reservation into several smaller reservations. When questioned as to why, the officials replied that it was to open up more land for white settlement. This time, the officials added, the Indians would be paid for any of the reservation land they sold.

## Broken Promises

For almost a year, all the tribes of the Great Sioux Nation resisted the offer, but in 1889, after veiled threats against them if they continued to hold out, most of the reservation Indians agreed to what the government wanted. They obediently packed up and moved to the smaller areas. James McLaughlin, the unpleasant government agent at Standing Rock Reservation, didn't even tell Sitting Bull about the meeting where the final agreement was to be signed by other Sioux leaders. When the elderly chief finally learned what had happened, he was very angry, telling everyone that the new smaller reservations would be like "an island in the middle of a sea [of white people]."

A newspaper photograph from the late 1800s features Major James McLaughlin, the government agent at Standing Rock Reservation. He did everything he possibly could to break Sitting Bull's spirit but never succeeded.

Sitting Bull even went so far as to confront McLaughlin about it, asking why the agent hadn't told him about the meeting. McLaughlin lied and said that he had, but that Sitting Bull must have just forgotten about it.

Following the Native Americans' move to the smaller reservations, severe droughts caused the crops to fail, and many families faced starvation. Sitting Bull told everyone who came to visit him, "We are ready to live the new life, but we cannot farm the soil as the agent [McLaughlin] wishes. Go look at our fields. Each year they are burned white by the sun. The leaves of the corn are even now rolled together. The wheat is beginning to

# Indian Reservations Today

An Indian reservation is land managed by a particular Native American tribe under the authority of the Department of the Interior's Bureau of Indian Affairs. Although the land is *federal* land, belonging to the U.S. government, the tribes have limited **sovereignty** over it. For instance, laws now permit legal gambling casinos on Indian land, and that attracts a lot of tourist money. These millions and millions of dollars have allowed many tribal members to enjoy a higher standard of living, an enormous change from the near subsistence way of living during Sitting Bull's time.

Today, there are about three hundred Indian reservations in the United States. Not all of the country's almost six hundred recognized tribes have a reservation, and some tribes have more than one. There are twelve reservations that are larger than the state of Rhode Island. Nine reservations are larger than the state of Delaware. Some states do not have reservations. Today, of course, Native Americans may live anywhere they wish in the United States, but many choose to stay on reservations because they believe it gives a certain cohesiveness to the tribe and helps it survive.

Many tribes today have built large casinos that bring in so much money that the standards of living for their people have been raised significantly. This photograph shows an Apache casino in Arizona.

dry up. There is no hay and the rations [the other food supplies from the U.S. government] are being cut down." With so little available food, the resistance of the Native people was low, and many died from different diseases such as measles, influenza, and whooping cough. To make matters worse, none of the Indians ever received the money that the government had promised them for their land. Once again, what the government had promised never materialized.

When people are presented with desperate situations, they often look for spiritual solutions, and although the Sioux still believed in *Wakan Tanka*, many of them had begun to think that the Great Spirit had abandoned them. Then on January 1, 1889, an event took place among the Paiute tribe in the southwestern part of the United States that would lift the spirits of all Native Americans and make them believe, once again, that they could rid their sacred lands of white people.

## Reawakened Spirits

As the story goes, Wovoka, a Paiute holy man, whose "white" name was Jack Wilson, had a vision during a **solar eclipse**. He was transported from Earth to the Spirit World and was given a sacred message. When he returned to Earth, he immediately spread the news of his vision. He said he was told that if his people performed the Ghost Dance, the Earth would be renewed and the buffalo and other wild game would return. Not only that, but all of the Indians who had been killed by the whites or had died from their diseases would also return, and the white people would disappear. There would no longer be sickness or unhappiness, and the tribes would live together in peace.

Although Wovoka's tribe lived far away from the Sioux, the news of their new religion spread quickly. In October 1890, a Miniconjou named Kicking Bear came to Sitting Bull's reservation to tell the Hunkpapa about the Ghost Dance. He convinced them that if they wore a special Ghost Shirt, the bullets used by the bluecoats would never harm them.

Almost all of the tribes west of the Mississippi River participated in the Ghost Dance ceremony to one degree or another. The Sioux, especially, believed that it would eventually allow them to return to their old ways. Before long, the Ghost Dance had become a very important part of the Hunkpapa's spiritual life. Wearing their Ghost Shirts, the members of the tribe would dance in a circle for five straight days, singing and praying to *Wakan Tanka* to bury all the white people in a mighty earthquake.

This lithograph from the 1890s depicts Sioux warriors performing the Ghost Dance.

Although Sitting Bull no longer believed that dead people could return to Earth, he allowed his followers to participate in the Ghost Dance. Since the great chief had a reputation as a holy man and the most important dance circle was on the banks of the Grand River, near where Sitting Bull lived, his involvement gave the movement credibility. Later, Sitting Bull began to hear rumors that the bluecoats didn't want the Indians doing the dance. It wasn't long before McLaughlin had Kicking Bear moved off the reservation.

Kicking Bear's removal didn't stop the Ghost Dance, though, and it actually served to anger Sitting Bull, because he believed his religious beliefs were nobody else's business but his. He told the government agents that he had noticed that the white people worshipped in different ways and that nobody was trying to stop them.

The Ghost Dance ceremony had truly reawakened the spirit of the Sioux, and they were all now totally convinced that it was the answer to their prayers. Although government officials and agents at the reservations thought the Ghost Dance was foolish, they were intelligent enough to know

*. . . he believed his religious beliefs were nobody else's business but his.*

that if the Indians really believed in what Wovoka's vision had promised, they might truly revolt and kill as many whites as they could. When settlers in nearby towns and villages began to fear an Indian insurrection, they demanded that the government give them protection from the dancers, and the Office of Indian Affairs was only too happy to comply. They sent more army troops to the area.

General Nelson Miles, the military commander in charge, made a list of the people on the reservation who were stirring up the Ghost Dancing groups, and Sitting Bull's name was at the top. A warrant was issued for his arrest. But Miles was unsure how to arrest Sitting Bull, because he knew the move would anger the great chief's followers. He eventually came up with an elaborate plan that called for Sitting Bull's friend, Buffalo Bill Cody, to take the chief into custody. McLaughlin was against the plan because he didn't want other government officials telling him how to do his job. He especially didn't appreciate how Cody had often tried to interfere with his authority at the reservation. McLaughlin sent a secret telegram to Washington, asking for the general's plan to be overridden, which it was. McLaughlin took great pleasure in letting Cody know that he was no longer needed.

Shortly afterward, McLaughlin issued a second arrest warrant for Sitting Bull.

# CHAPTER 14

# The Death of Sitting Bull

*If the white men want me to die, they ought not to put up the Indians to kill me.*

In November 1890, Sitting Bull, now almost sixty years old, went out into the country, a few miles from his cabin, to look for the horse that Buffalo Bill had given him. He was no longer able to ride the animal as much as he once did, journeying throughout the sacred land. About three miles out, he came upon the steed grazing peacefully, so he sat under a tree while the horse continued to feed. A few minutes later, Sitting Bull heard a voice, and then he saw a meadowlark land on a nearby tree branch. The bird was looking directly at Sitting Bull, moving its beak up and down, not singing but telling him over and over that his own people were going to end his life. He immediately felt a tremendous sadness and wanted to forget the meadowlark's words, but if he did, he would be going against the wishes of *Wakan Tanka*, who had sent the bird to him. Sitting Bull knew only too well how to interpret the meadowlark's message.

Agent McLaughlin had been increasing his police force by hiring Indians from the reservation. They were known as *Ceska Maza*, a Sioux phrase meaning "Metal Breasts." Sitting Bull was sure the meadowlark meant that the Metal Breasts would be the ones to kill him.

This 1889 photograph shows three Sioux policemen, known as Metal Breasts because of the metal badges they wore.

## An Early Morning Arrest

A few weeks later, McLaughlin became alarmed when Sitting Bull announced that he was planning to visit some old friends at the Pine Ridge Reservation to the south.

Just before dawn on December 15, 1890, a few days before Sitting Bull was to leave for Pine Ridge, forty-three Metal Breasts approached Sitting Bull's cabin on the Grand River. Bull Head, one of the Metal Breast lieutenants, entered first and found Sitting Bull naked and sleeping on the floor. Bull Head shook Sitting Bull's shoulder to awaken the old chief. He told the dazed Indian to get up, because he was now a prisoner and was being taken to McLaughlin at agency headquarters.

In 1890, Sitting Bull was dragged from this cabin. This c. 1891 photograph shows some of Sitting Bull's family members sitting on the front steps.

At first, in the confusion of being so abruptly awakened, Sitting Bull didn't understand what was happening. When it finally dawned on him, he told Bull Head he would go with him without a struggle as soon as he could put on some clothes. It was important to Sitting Bull that he maintain some of his dignity in the situation.

In the meantime, Sitting Bull's son, Crow Foot, who was in the cabin with his father, escaped through the back door. He immediately raced toward the cabins of the other Hunkpapa to let them know what the Metal Breasts were doing. Although the other Indian policemen saw Crow Foot leaving, they weren't able to stop him. They quickly told Bull Head they were sure the boy had gone to get some of Sitting Bull's followers. The Metal Breasts now demanded that Sitting Bull dress more quickly.

# Indian Policemen

When the United States government created Indian reservations, military troops were given the authority to maintain order. Then in 1877, Ezra A. Hayt, Commissioner of Indian Affairs, urged the government to create a system of Indian policemen who would answer to the agent of the reservation and replace the military. For Hayt, this seemed like the perfect first step to integrating the Indian population into American society. By 1890, almost sixty of the reservations had an Indian police force. The success of the system was due to the fact that the police force often replaced the tribal society, which had previously played the same kind of law-and-order role. This was especially true for the Sioux where an Indian policeman was the highest-ranking tribal member.

This photograph from the late 1890s shows mounted Sioux policemen called Metal Breasts.

When Sitting Bull failed to speed it up, the Metal Breasts grabbed him by the arms and pulled him, half-dressed, out of the cabin. The angry old man shouted at them to release him and said he would go without their help, but the Metal Breasts continued to push him around. By now, numerous Hunkpapa from the other cabins were beginning to surround the Metal Breasts who had themselves encircled Sitting Bull's cabin. Sitting Bull's followers were angrily shouting at the Metal Breasts, telling them to release their great chief or the Metal Breasts themselves would be killed.

## One Last Act of Resistance

Hearing the shouts of his family members and supporters, Sitting Bull suddenly found a strength he thought had left him in his old age. Thinking about what would happen to his people if he were not there with them reminded him that he had always been a great warrior and that he couldn't stop being one now. To the Metal Breasts, he said, "You are all Indians, and the blood that runs in your veins is the same as mine—you are my own people. I have repeatedly cautioned all Indians to have no faith in the government. I have refused to give our lands away. Now . . . [our lands] are gone and we have received no pay. My own children now come as agents of that government to arrest me and stand ready to shoot down their own flesh and blood to assist that government. You have no right to do this. You are cowards to come to my house in the nighttime. You are dogs to raise your hands against your own people, and you do not deserve to be called [Sioux] or to live. I call upon my friends to kill you now."

Sitting Bull's words fell on deaf ears, and several Metal Breasts began dragging the old chief toward a horse. At that moment, one of Sitting Bull's bodyguards, Catch-the-Bear, aimed his rifle and fired at Bull Head. As Bull Head collapsed, he aimed his gun and fired at Sitting Bull, striking him in the chest. Almost at the same time, Red Tomahawk released Sitting Bull's arm, drew his gun, and shot Sitting Bull in the head. The great chief fell to the ground, dead.

Sitting Bull's followers rushed the Metal Breasts. They fought with one another for the next several minutes, until the cavalry arrived and separated the two groups. Besides Sitting Bull, eight Hunkpapa died in the battle, including Crow Foot. Six Metal Breasts also died.

This 1897 photograph is of Red Tomahawk, who was considered a celebrity because he was credited with killing Sitting Bull. He was often invited to Washington, D.C., as a guest of North Dakota politicians.

This lithograph from the late 1890s claims to show the ensuing battle between Sitting Bull's followers and the U.S. Cavalry and Metal Breasts after Sitting Bull was killed.

Sitting Bull was buried without dignity at Fort Yates, North Dakota. Since there were no friends or family allowed at the funeral, it remained for some U.S. soldier-prisoners from the post guardhouse to lower Sitting Bull's wooden casket into the ground. Officials in Washington, D.C., believed that with Sitting Bull's death, the struggle with the Sioux would come to an end. They couldn't have been more wrong.

## The Massacre at Wounded Knee

Without their leader, the remaining Hunkpapa left their homes on the Grand River and joined up with Big Foot's tribe, the Miniconjou. As a chief, Big Foot was considered a man of peace and was known for his skill at settling quarrels. In many ways,

A modern monument marks Sitting Bull's gravesite at Fort Yates, North Dakota.

he reminded the Hunkpapa of Sitting Bull. Before long, though, the bluecoats found them and forced them to set up another camp on the banks of a creek called Wounded Knee.

Before his death, Sitting Bull had made it clear to the government agents that he wouldn't stand for any interference in his religious practices, namely the Ghost Dance. The other Great Plains Indians also echoed that if the whites interfered, they could count on violent resistance. The Indians would meet force with force, fire with fire.

For their part, the whites were sure that these were not idle threats from the Indians. Almost daily, there were rumors that the Sioux were on the warpath, that they had already been attacking farms and villages, and were killing every white person they encountered. None of this was true, but it didn't matter, because the white settlers in the region wanted to believe it. Newspapers in the region printed all of these rumors without ever trying to discover if there was any truth to them. The white settlers who saw in bold headlines what they already believed anyway were whipped to a fever pitch and began calling for **preemptive strikes** by the army. Why should we wait until the Indians have killed some of our loved ones? Why don't we just kill them all first?

On December 29, Colonel George Forsyth from the Pine Ridge Reservation ordered his troops to surround the Sioux camp at Wounded Knee. Forsyth ordered the men and older boys to come out and sit in a semicircle in the deep snow facing the guns.

Next, Colonel Forsyth ordered some of his men to search the tepees for anything suspicious but especially for guns. Inside, the soldiers found the women and the younger children cowering in

*Officials in Washington, D.C., believed that with Sitting Bull's death, the struggle with the Sioux would come to an end.*

fear. When some of the men started shoving the women around to get them out of their way, the children started wailing so loudly that the men and older boys became agitated. They knew that if they moved, though, the bullets from the machine guns would kill them instantly.

Yellow Bird, a medicine man living in the camp, suddenly got up and began doing the Ghost Dance. As he danced, Yellow Bird reminded the men and older boys that the Ghost Shirts they were wearing would make them safe from the bullets of the bluecoats.

Colonel George Forsyth was in command of the troops at the Wounded Knee
Massacre on December 29, 1890. This photograph shows him in the late 1860s.

Suddenly, a random shot rang out. Some accounts say the
shot came from a deaf Indian named Black Coyote, who was
struggling with a soldier trying to take his gun away. As the
terrified Sioux ran first one way, then another, trying to escape
the hail of bullets, they were all killed. Their bodies fell into
grotesque positions. When at last it was over, the soldiers
searched the Sioux for souvenirs. They especially wanted to find
Ghost Shirts with bullet holes in them. Eventually, the bodies
were buried together in one communal grave. This massacre at

American troops line trenches as Sioux men, women, and children are put into a mass grave after the Wounded Knee Massacre on December 29, 1890.

Wounded Knee was the last major engagement between the Indians of the plains and the U.S. Army.

## Sitting Bull's Legacy

Away from Wounded Knee, on the other reservations, the remaining Sioux remembered what Sitting Bull had once said while he was fighting so hard to keep his way of life alive: "Is it wicked of me because my skin is red; because I am a Lakota [Sioux]; because I was born where my fathers lived; because I would die for my people and country?"

Sadly, the answer seemed to be "yes" in the eyes of the white men who battled the Sioux in their attempt to expand the West.

A statue of Sitting Bull on the campus of the University of North Dakota captures the strong will of this Sioux chief.

But to his people, Sitting Bull was their great leader—a Sioux chief of the largest Native American group on the North American continent. He sacrificed everything to keep the U.S. government from taking over his people's sacred homeland. Even in death, Sitting Bull's values and principles guided his tribe. His fight to attain justice for his people has become one of the most inspiring Native American stories in the history of the American West.

# Glossary

**allied**—united in a close relationship.

**cavalry**—soldiers trained to fight on horseback.

**column of troops**—a formation in which all soldiers follow one behind the other.

**decimating**—reducing drastically in number. For instance, killing a large group of animals.

**demeaned**—shamed or lowered in dignity.

**democracy**—government system in which all citizens of a country have the right to participate.

**geologists**—people who study the origin, history, and structure of the Earth.

**muzzle-loading guns**—guns loaded by pouring a measured amount of gunpowder down the barrel and then ramming a metal ball (bullet) on top of the gunpowder.

**neutrality**—not taking sides in a conflict.

**nomadic**—moving from place to place with no permanent home.

**novitiate**—a place for a man who has entered a religious order but who has not yet taken the final vows to become a priest.

**pigments**—dry natural color substances that can be used for paint when mixed with water.

**preemptive strikes**—military strikes against an enemy before the enemy can attack them.

**prisoners of war**—people who are captured and imprisoned by an enemy during a war.

**rawhide**—dried skin of an animal used for making ropes.

**renegades**—people who reject one group for another.

**rest on their laurels**—being satisfied with what they have achieved and deciding that no further effort is needed.

**scavengers**—animals that feed on dead or decaying matter.

**seceded**—formally withdrew, as a state from the United States.

**solar eclipse**—an event that occurs when the moon passes between the sun and the Earth so that the sun is wholly or partially obscured.

**sovereignty**—the power or rule over something.

**strategy**—plan of action.

**trance**—a dazed state between sleeping and waking.

# Bibliography

**Books**

Diedrich, Mark, ed. *Sitting Bull: The Collected Speeches*. Rochester, Minnesota: Coyote Books, 1998.

Eisenberg, Lisa. *The Story of Sitting Bull, Great Sioux Chief*. New York: Bantam Doubleday Dell, 1991.

Garland, Hamlin. *The Book of the American Indian*. New York: Harper and Brother, 1923.

Turner, John Peter. *The North-West Mounted Police, 1873–1893. 2 vols.* Ottawa: King's Printer and Controller of Stationary, 1950.

Utley, Robert M. *The Lance and the Shield: The Life and Times of Sitting Bull*. New York: Random House, 1993.

Vestal, Stanley. *Sitting Bull, Champion of the Sioux*. Norman, Oklahoma: University of Oklahoma Press, 1932.

**Articles**

*New York Times*, "The Indians," July 1, 1871.

Stirling, Matthew W. *Three Pictographic Autobiographies of Sitting Bull*. Washington, D.C.: Smithsonian Miscellaneous Collections 97, July 22, 1938.

# Source Notes

The following list contains citations for the sources of the quoted material found in this book. The first and last few words of each quotation are cited and followed by its source. Complete information on referenced sources can be found in the Bibliography.

**Abbreviations:**

**BAI**—*The Book of the American Indian*

**LATS**—*The Lance and the Shield: The Life and Times of Sitting Bull*

**NYT**—*The New York Times* (article dated July 1, 1871)

**SBCS**—*Sitting Bull: The Collected Speeches*

**SBCOTS**—*Sitting Bull, Champion of the Sioux*

**TPAOSB**—*Three Pictographic Autobiographies of Sitting Bull*

**INTRODUCTION: He Lived and Died for His People**
   PAGE 1 *"I wish . . . my rifle."*: SBCS, p. 139

**CHAPTER 1: The Greatest Gift**
   PAGE 2 *"When I was . . . their lands."*: SBCS, p. 58
   PAGE 3 *"I began . . . my people."*: SBCS, p. 60

**CHAPTER 2: Becoming a Warrior**
   PAGE 11 *"I was born . . . draw a bow."*: SBCS, p. 58
   PAGE 17 *"When I was ten . . . of the tribe."*: SBCS, p. 59

**CHAPTER 3: His Name Is Now Sitting Bull**
   PAGE 18 *"I kill . . . for food."*: BAI, p. 173

**CHAPTER 4: A Message from *Wakan Tanka***
   PAGE 24 *"I am satisfied . . . am I here?"*: SBCS, p. 19

**CHAPTER 5: Becoming a Leader**
   PAGE 32 *"I tell you . . . nothing bad."*: SBCS, p. 38
   PAGE 39 *"[It] took [a] . . . in that fight."*: TPAOSB, p. 44
   PAGE 40 *"Big brother!"*: SBCOTS, p. 36

**CHAPTER 6: The Movement West**
   PAGE 42 *"I do not . . . to invade ours."*: BAI, p. 165

# Image Credits

# About the Author

George E. Stanley received his doctorate in African linguistics from the University of Port Elizabeth in South Africa. He is now Professor of African and Middle-Eastern Languages and Linguistics at Cameron University in Lawton, Oklahoma, where he teaches Arabic, Persian, Swahili, and Urdu. He is also a well-known children's author, with one hundred books to his credit, including several critically acclaimed biographies.

# Index